CONSERVATORY CANADA

GUITAR SYLLABUS 1999 Edition
Effective 1 September 1998
(Reprinted November 1999)

This Syllabus replaces all previous guitar syllabi of both Western Ontario Conservatory of Music and The Western Board of Music, and will remain in effect until further notice.

Guitar Syllabus Committee

Claudia Chalk, Surrey, BC
Kevin Love, London, ON

Contents

Introduction

Conservatory Canada examination programs provide a new nation-wide system for evaluation and accreditation, through core programs to encourage and assess broadly-based musicianship. As well, there are innovative features (such as Mini-Lessons, and Recital Assessments) that increase the options for flexibility, educational value, and meaningful and friendly interaction among teacher, student and examiner.

While this syllabus is not intended as a curriculum (that's the prerogative of the teacher), it is designed to give guidance and support to teachers and their students, with built-in opportunity where possible to serve those with broader experience or varying needs.

The clearly-defined goals of an examination encourage comprehensive skill development, and offer an arms-length assessment of progress against a national standard. While the examination forms a valuable part of a total picture of musical training, it should not be considered as the entire focus of music studies. *Teachers are urged to explore a wide variety of repertoire in lessons throughout the year, and then to choose from this the pieces that will be performed in the examination.* Conservatory Canada believes that the practical examination must assess as broad a spectrum of skills and musicianship as possible. So, in addition to pieces and studies, we devote significant focus to technique, aural and sight training, oral questions, and, in the higher grades, to skills in harmonization. Students trained in all these disciplines will be prepared to address with confidence whatever musical challenges await them in later life.

List Pieces & Studies
List pieces have been chosen to give a representative sampling of composers and styles. Provision for Supplementary Pieces and Irregular Lists allow for the use of works not included in this Syllabus but which may be favorites of the teacher or student. The Twentieth-Century lists offer unparalleled selection and variety.

Technique
Technical requirements, including the sequence of keys, are carefully paced to help prepare for repertoire demands in each grade. Nevertheless, we have sought to balance training needs against the realities of time limitations in the lesson and varying student commitment. Conservatory Canada's *Guitar Technique Book* (1999) includes all required scales, triads and arpeggios, notated grade by grade, with suggested fingerings. Where feasible, new concepts and exercises are introduced gradually, in a few keys at first, to develop basic skills without adding extra volume of work. With scales and triads, a modest review process re-visits, on a revolving basis, several keys from earlier grades to keep them current and to reduce the time spent relearning them in later grades where all keys are required. Provision is made for a taste of whole-tone, pentatonic, and blues scales, each in one or two keys only, in Grades 5-7, not so much for technical development as to expand the student's awareness of 20th-century and multicultural sounds. They're useful tools for composing and improvising, too.

Harmonization Skills
The ability to perform chord progressions and harmonization was a standard expectation of every musician in the Baroque period. And it is still of great value today for composers, jazz musicians, and accompanists. These skills, often intimidating for teachers but enjoyed by curious students, are introduced very gradually beginning at Grade 5.

Viva Voce
Oral questions about pieces, titles, terms, forms, and composers in examinations up to and including Grade 8 encourage general musical knowledge and understanding of the styles and specific works performed. Written History and Theory co-requisites take over this function in Grades 9 and 10.

The Guitar Syllabus Committee hopes that this graded Syllabus will serve to invite exploration of new repertoire, build musicianship skills, and provide a yardstick to measure progress from year to year.

GENERAL INFORMATION & REGULATIONS

This syllabus contains regulations and requirements for piano examinations for Grades 1 to 10. For Associate (Teacher and Performer) Diploma and Licentiate Diploma requirements, see the Associate/Licentiate syllabus.

Subjects

Examinations are offered in the following subject areas:

Practical

Piano (classical and Contemporary Idioms)
Voice (classical and Contemporary Idioms)
Guitar (classical and Contemporary Idioms)
Violin, Viola, Violoncello
Flute, Clarinet, Saxophone
Trumpet, French Horn, Trombone, Tuba
Teacher Development
Recital Assessment

Written

Theory 1	History 5	Pedagogy
Theory 2	History 6	
Theory 3	History 7	
Theory 4		
Theory 5		
Theory 6		
Theory 7A & 7B		

SESSIONS

Practical Examinations

CONSERVATORY CANADA™ conducts three practical examination sessions during each academic year. These session include most instruments and voice, and are held at centres throughout Canada. New centres may be established by arrangement with the Conservatory.

WINTER	last two weeks in February	
	(application deadline is normally early November)	
SPRING	the entire month of June	
	(application deadline is normally early March)	
SUMMER	last two weeks of August	
	(application deadline is normally early July)	

Applicants should consult the website for the specific deadline date
of the session for which they wish to apply.

eExams

CONSERVATORY CANADA™ also offers eExams: these examinations are conducted online whenever the student is ready. Many eExam centres are set up across the country. Please contact our office for more details on this convenient option.

Flex Exams

Under special circumstances, CONSERVATORY CANADA™ may be able to offer Flex Exams. These take place outside of the normal exam session dates, and are only feasible where there is access to a local Examiner who has no knowledge of the candidate(s) involved, and there is access to a no-cost venue for hosting the examination. Enquiries for Flex Exams must be made through the Conservatory office.

Scheduling

CONSERVATORY CANADA™ offers an online application service for examination applications. For convenience, many of our large centres offer online scheduling allowing students to choose the day and time for their exam. For those centres that do not have online scheduling, we make every effort to schedule examinations around legitimate events such as school trips or school examinations, provided notice is given at the time of application (included in the application process). However, because of constraints in reserving facilities and examiners, this cannot be guaranteed.

For candidates who do not have access to our online scheduling service, the Registrar will schedule exams manually and notification will be made available through the teacher and student portals. Notification providing date, time and location will be available at least two weeks prior to the practical examination. Candidates and their teachers are not permitted to change dates or times of the scheduled examination except through the Office of the Registrar.

Written Examinations

CONSERVATORY CANADA™ conducts three written examination sessions during each academic year.

WINTER	second Saturday in January
	(application deadline is normally early November)
SPRING	second Saturday in May
	(application deadline is normally early March)
SUMMER	second Saturday in August
	(application deadline is normally late June)

Flex Written Exams

CONSERVATORY CANADA™ also offers Flex Written Exams: candidates are able to schedule, in consultation with the Registrar, an examination date outside of the regular examination sessions. Please contact our office for more details on this convenient option.

Applications

Candidates are encouraged to apply for examinations online at our website www.conservatorycanada.ca. Paper applications are available for download from the site, and a handling fee of $25 will be added. A separate application is required for each examination. When registering for an examination, ensure that you have your teacher's ID number from the conservatory database. It is important that, once you have a candidate number from the system, the same number be used for all future examination transactions.

Centres

Practical examinations are conducted by qualified examiners appointed by CONSERVATORY CANADA™ in centres where there are enough candidates registered to warrant sending an examiner. If we are unable to send an Examiner, candidates have the following options:

- eExams (practical evaluations conducted online)
- Travel to the nearest viable centre

Candidates should plan to arrive at least 15 minutes before the examination is scheduled to begin.

Appeals

Queries or appeals concerning the examination procedure must be filed in writing with the Office of the Registrar within 10 days of the completion of the examination.

Cancellations

Notice of withdrawal, for any reason, must be submitted in writing to the Office of the Registrar. Consult the **Cancellation Policies & Regulations** information found on our website.

Marking Standards

The marking standard of CONSERVATORY CANADA™ is as follows:

First-Class Honours with Distinction:	90 – 100 marks
First-Class Honours:	80 – 89
Honours:	70 – 79
Pass:	60 – 69
Insufficient to Pass:	Below 60 marks

Results and Notices

All examination notices, results and certificates are available online at www.conservatorycanada.ca through the teacher and student portals. Under no condition will examination results be released verbally, either in person or by telephone. Because examination marks are confidential to the teacher and candidate, results cannot be released to any other person.

Transfer Credits

Transfer credit is not possible for practical subjects. However, candidates who have successfully completed equivalent examinations in Theory and History courses at recognized conservatories and/or universities may apply for transfer credit. If approved, the transfer credit can be used to satisfy the co-requisite requirement for the awarding of a practical certificate.

- To apply for a transcript evaluation with a view to obtaining transfer credit, candidates must arrange to have an official transcript sent by the issuing institution direct to the CONSERVATORY CANADA™ office.
- Candidates must email the office at mail@conservatorycanada.ca indicating the desired transfer. Further details for transfer can be found on our website

SCHOLARSHIPS AND AWARDS

Endowed Scholarships
The annual interest earned by CONSERVATORY CANADA™ Scholarship Endowment Funds allows us to award scholarships totaling more than $30,000. These scholarships are awarded based on varying criteria (found on our website).

CONSERVATORY CANADA™ is a not-for-profit organization (charitable number 891687121RR0001). We welcome and are grateful for any donations and sponsorships in support of any of our programs. For further details on how you can help foster the importance of music study for children and adults of every age, contact our office at 1-800-461-5367, www.conservatorycanada.ca and use the convenient *DONATE NOW* link.

Prizes and Awards
From time to time donations are received and are to be given as prizes and awards. These are awarded as stipulated by the donor and presented directly to the student.

Certificates
Certificates are awarded for all practical, theory and history examinations upon the successful completion of all requirements. For practical examinations in Grades/levels 5 to 10, certificates will be issued conditional upon the completion of theory/history co-requisite requirements listed for each Grade/level. Certificates are available for printing from the student and teacher portals.

Medals for Excellence
Medals will be awarded to the candidate who receives the highest mark (minimum mark of 85%) in each Grade for each province for the academic year. Medals are awarded in each practical instrument area (Classical and Contemporary Idioms), as well as for theory and history. To be eligible, candidates must complete the examination in one sitting, and also must have completed all of the prescribed theory and history co-requisites, if appropriate. Candidates who are considered to be professional musicians and candidates who take partial or supplemental examinations are not eligible for medals.

Academic Credits
CONSERVATORY CANADA™ examination candidates may be eligible for Secondary School external credits according to the requirements as outlined by the various provincial Ministries of Education. This criteria can be viewed on our website.

Visually Impaired or Physically Challenged Candidates
Special provisions can be made for visually-impaired or physically challenged candidates. For details, please contact the Office of the Registrar before the closing date for applications.

REGULATIONS FOR PRACTICAL EXAMINATIONS

Conduct of Practical Examinations

Only the Examiner, or Examiners, and the candidate will be permitted to be present in the examination room during the progress of the examination. Where piano accompanists are needed, they will be permitted in the room only for those portions for which their services are required.

Recording equipment is not permitted in the examination room.

In accordance with copyright law, photocopies of musical scores (for use by the candidate or accompanist or the examiner) are NOT permitted in the examination room unless the candidate can present written authorization from the copyright holder. The examiner has been instructed NOT to proceed with the examination while unauthorized photocopies are present.

Candidates must list in the appropriate place on the back of the examination notice all repertoire to be performed in the examination. This list must be given to the examiner at the start of the examination.

Editions

Any standard edition of the music may be used for the examination. However, candidates are encouraged to choose editions that represent the composer's intentions in the clearest, and most straightforward manner. Candidates may NOT use simplified or adapted versions of works to be performed.

Irregular Lists

Any piece not found in the list pieces for the particular grade in this syllabus constitutes an irregular list piece.

Candidates may make written request, by mail, fax or in person, to the Office of the Registrar for approval to perform a maximum of ONE irregular list piece.

Requests for approval must include full details of the piece along with a copy of the music, and must reach the Registrar's Office at least 30 days before the deadline for application. The Conservatory cannot take responsibility if the request is denied and the piece deemed inappropriate for the examination.

For those pieces given special approval, an official form setting this out will be sent to the candidate who must, in turn, hand it along with the printed score to the Examiner at the time of the examination.

A piece approved as an irregular list piece may not be played at a subsequent examination.

NOTE: It is permissible, without special approval, to include one piece from the next higher grade in this Syllabus, providing it is from the same list. Compositions listed in this Syllabus for more than one grade higher may NOT be used.

Partial Examinations

Candidates in Grades 8, 9 and 10 may choose to take the examination in two parts, each at a different session. These partial examinations are to be divided into two reasonably equals parts, each part comprising approximately 50% of the marks allotted for that grade (see MARKS at the end of each grade). The first part must contain no less than 44% and no more than 56% of the requirements. The second part must be completed within twelve months following the first sitting, and must include all aspects not previously examined in the first part.

The division of the examination is left to the discretion of the teacher and candidate. Sections given a composite mark (*e.g.* the complete technical requirements or the complete aural tests) may not be sub-divided and must be completed at one sitting. At each sitting the list presented to the Examiner must contain details of all components that are to be heard. Each section as it is presented will be awarded a mark.

No portion of a partial examination completed during the first sitting may be repeated for the second sitting in order to attempt to improve the mark already awarded.

The total mark at the conclusion of the second sitting determines the standing of the candidate, and there can be no recourse to adjustment of this final mark. If the results of the first sitting are low, then it might be to the advantage of the candidate to start over.

Candidates who choose to play a partial examination will not be eligible for either scholarships or medals.

Theory & History Co-requisites For Practical Certificates

Theoretical subjects are required for practical Certificates for all instruments and voice beyond Grade 4. Certificates are issued only when the required Theory and/or History co-requisites are completed. Candidates are strongly urged to complete all written co-requisites before entering for the practical examination. Co-requisites must be successfully completed within ten years of completion of the practical examinations. No certificate will be awarded after this period has lapsed.

It is recognized that, in some cases, Western Ontario Conservatory and/or Western Board courses do not have exactly the same content as the Conservatory Canada equivalent. Nevertheless, in the interest of convenience and fairness, the equivalents (along with the various written co-requisites for each grade in all instruments and voice) given below will be considered as having covered the same material.

THEORY & HISTORY CO-REQUISITES FOR PRACTICAL CERTIFICATES

Practical Grade	WOCM Theory (before 1999)	Western Board Theory (before 1999)	New Syllabus Theory (beginning in 1999)
1	No requirement	No requirement	No requirement
2	No requirement	No requirement	No requirement
3	No requirement	No requirement	No requirement
4	No requirement	No requirement	No requirement
5	Introductory Rudiments	Grade 1 (Rudiments)	Theory 1
6	Rudiments 1	Grade 2 (Rudiments)	Theory 2
7	Rudiments 2	Grade 3 (Rudiments)	Theory 3
8	Rudiments 2	Grade 4 (Rudiments)	Theory 4
9	Harmony 3 ----- History 3	Grade 5 (Harmony) Grade 5 (Aural) -----	Theory 5 NOT required History 5 OR 6 [your choice]
10	Harmony 4 Counterpoint 4 ----- ----- History 3 History 4	Grade 6 (Harmony) ----- Grade 6 (Form & Analysis) Grade 6 (Aural) ----- Grade 6 (History)	Theory 6 [included in Theory 6] [included in Theory 6] NOT required History 5 History 6
Associate (performer)	Combined Harmony 5 Form & Analysis 5 History 5	----- Grade 7 (Form & Analysis) Grade 7 (History)	Theory 7A (Harmony/Counterpoint) Theory 7B (Form & Analysis) History 7
Associate (teacher)	Combined Harmony 5 Form & Analysis 5 History 5 Pedagogy	----- Grade 7 (Form & Analysis) Grade 7 (History) Pedagogy	Theory 7A (Harmony/Counterpoint) Theory 7B (Form & Analysis) History 7 Pedagogy 7

Candidates who have completed successfully Theory and History examinations at the August 1998 session or earlier under either The Western Board syllabus or Western Ontario Conservatory syllabus may use these equivalent credits to satisfy the co-requisites for the awarding of a practical certificate as outlined in this syllabus.

For details concerning regulations and requirements for all Rudiments/Theory and History examinations, candidates should consult the new *Theory & History Syllabus (1998)*. This syllabus must be used beginning with the January 1999 written examination session.

Mini-Lessons

Mini-Lessons provide a unique learning opportunity for students at all grade levels and, at the same time, serve as an informal, private workshop for the teacher. It is an optional 15-minute private lesson, with the teacher present, to be given by the examiner immediately following the practical examination. The Mini-Lesson will not be used to review any aspect of the candidate's performance in the preceeding examination, but rather it may be used to explore ways to overcome particular technical difficulties or investigate ideas concerning musicianship and style relating to proposed new pieces or studies to help the candidate prepare for the next year. Mini-Lessons are tailored to the needs of the student, and to this end, the teacher and/or the student may wish to suggest to the examiner what they would like to cover in the Mini-Lesson. Candidates wishing to register for a Mini-Lesson should indicate this in the appropriate place on the examination application form and also enclose the appropriate Mini-Lesson fee.

INSTRUCTIONS FOR GUITAR CANDIDATES

1. For those grades where a separate mark is given for memory, full marks will be awarded only when each of the pieces is memorized accurately. Full marks will not be awarded for performances that need re-starts or include stumbles, nor for performances where the musical score is used. Candidates are required to memorize all List Pieces and the prescribed technical requirements (see the technique section for the specific grade). In Grade 10, where a separate mark is not given for memory, candidates can expect a deduction of up to 10% for work that is not properly memorized.

2. Any logical and satisfactory system of fingering may be used in any part of the examination. However, unorthodox systems may be open to criticism by the Examiner if they adversely affect accuracy, rhythm, consistency of touch and musicality in general.

3. Candidates in *Grades 1-4 inclusive* must play ALL repeats. No repeats are to be played in Grades 5-10 unless they are essential to the musical sense of the piece (*e.g.* a Baroque dance or a Classical minuet & trio). However, *Da Capo* and *Dal Segno* indications must always be observed.

4. Metronome markings are given in each grade for the performance of the various technical tests. These speeds should be regarded as minimum tempi.

5. The candidate must provide the examiner with an original printed copy of all pieces to be performed.

6. Candidates in Grades 1-4 may ask the examiner for assistance in tuning their guitar. Candidates in Grade 5 and beyond are expected to tune their own instrument without assistance.

7. Candidates must provide their own foot stool and music stand (if one is required).

PUBLICATIONS

The authorized book for technical exercises is

    Guitar Technique Book, edited by Kevin Love, published by Novus Via Music Group (2014). Copies may be ordered from the Conservatory or from your local music retailer.

James McDaniel's *40 Compositions in Standard Real Book Form*, published by the composer (1996). Copies may be ordered from James B. McDaniel, 641 Viewcrest Drive, Dundee, Oregan, 97115, U.S.A. or from the Conservatory.

Steven Fielder's *Introduction to Keyboard Harmony and Transposition*, published by Waterloo Music (1993), contains graded melodies for harmonization that will prove useful for both keyboard and guitar players. Copies may be ordered from the published, or the Conservatory, or your local music retailer.

While there are many textbooks available that can be used to prepare for examinations in aural, sight reading and *viva voce* sections, candidates should check carefully all requirements in this Syllabus well in advance of the examination.

                    ————————————————

Candidates are expected to know all of the current regulations and requirements for the examinations as outlined in this Syllabus. No allowance can be made for candidates who misread or fail to follow any of the regulations and/or requirements for the examination.

Length of the examination: 20 minutes

Examination Fee: Please consult the current examination application form
                               for the schedule of fees.

Co-requisite   None. There is NO written examination co-requisite for the
                               awarding of the Grade 1 Practical Certificate.

Requirements & Marking

Requirement	Total Marks
TWO LIST PIECES To be performed from memory 1 2	 14 14
ONE STUDY	12
ONE SUPPLEMENTARY PIECE	10
TECHNICAL TESTS Scales & Triads Harmonization	 14 4
SIGHT READING Rhythm Pattern Guitar Passage	 3 7
AURAL TESTS	10
VIVA VOCE	6
MARKS FOR MEMORY List pieces only (3 marks each)	6
TOTAL POSSIBLE MARKS	100

Pieces
Candidates must be prepared to play TWO pieces from the following list, chosen to contrast in style, key, tempo, etc.. Your choice must include TWO different composers. All pieces must be performed from memory.

GRADE 1

LIST PIECES

ANONYMOUS
The Student Repertoire Book, I   Guitar Solo Pub
   Choose ANY ONE of
     Alla en la Fuente
     Lavenedero Blues
BEAUVAIS, W.
   Via Brazil   Harris
CARCASSI, M.
   Andantino in C   Colombo
   (Classic Guitar Technique, 1)
CARULLI, F./BREVIER
   Carulli/Brevier, I   Schott (GA)
   Choose ANY ONE of
     Poco Allegretto, Op. 246, No. 1
     Andante, Op. 246, No. 2
     Walzer, Op. 121 No. 1
     Anglaise, Op. 121 No. 6
     Walze, Op. 211 No. 2
   No. 2 *(18 Piccoli Pezzi, Op. 211)*   Berben
GAGNON, C.
   La guitar Enchantée   Doberman
   Choose ANY ONE of
     Chanson triste
     Chansonvieilotte
GIULIANI M./CHIESA
   Twelve Ecossaise Op. 33   Zerboni
   Choose ANY ONE of
     Nos. 2, 4, 6, 10

KOSHKIN, N.
   Mascarades for Guitar   Lemoine Music
   Choose ANY ONE of
     Goldfish
     Minstrel Song
     Pinocchio
     Colombine
     Paper Boat
     Rodeo
SANZ, G.
   Instruccion de Musica Sobre
   La Guitarra Española, I   Bitetti
   Choose ANY ONE of
     Mariona
     Españoleta
SHEARER, A.
   Classic Guitar Technique, I   Colombo
   Choose ANY ONE of
     Folk Song
     Prelude 15
     Prelude 16
TANSMAN, A.
   Douze pieces faciles, I   Eschig
   Choose ANY ONE of
     No. I Promenade
     No. II Ostinato
TRADITIONAL
   Concepts   Big 3 Music
   Choose ANY ONE of
     Syncopated Lamb
     Lamb Stew

Studies

Candidates must be prepared to play ONE study chosen from the following list. Memorization is recommended though NOT required.

STUDY LIST

AGUADO, D.
   Studi per Chitarra   Zerboni
   Choose ANY ONE of
     Nos. 2, 3
   8 Lessons for Guitar   Columbia Music
     No. 2
COSTE, N.
   First Studies   Universal
     No. 7
GIULIANI, M.
   Studi Per Chitarra, Op. 30   Zerboni
   Choose ANY ONE of
     Nos. 2, 13, 14

SAGRERAS, J.
   Las Primeras Lecciones   Ricordi
   Choose ANY ONE of
     Nos. 46, 52, 56, 60, 63, 66
SHEARER, A.
   Classic Guitar Technique, I   Colombo
   Choose ANY ONE of
     Etudes 9, 11, 12
SOR, F.
   Studi per Chitarra Op. 60, III   Zerboni
   Choose ANY ONE of
     Nos. 2, 8

Supplementary Piece

Candidates must be prepared to play ONE Supplementary Piece. This piece need not be from the Syllabus lists, and may be chosen entirely at the discretion of the teacher and student. It may represent a period or style of piece not already included in the examination program, but which holds special interest for the candidate. The choice must be within the following guidelines:

1) The equivalent level of difficulty of the piece may be at a higher grade level, providing it is within the technical and musical grasp of the candidate.

2) Pieces at the pre-grade 1 level are acceptable.

3) The piece must be for solo guitar. Duets and trios are not acceptable.

4) Candidates with exceptional talent for improvisation may wish to improvise upon a theme of their choice. In this case, items 1 and 2 (above) will apply. Marks will be given for originality, musical inventiveness, and structural unity.

Special approval is not required for the Supplementary Piece. However, poor suitability of the choice may be reflected in the mark. Memorization is encouraged, though NOT required.

Technical Tests

Conservatory Canada's booklet *Guitar Technique Book* (1999) contains notational examples for all technical requirements.

All technical tests must be played from memory, evenly, with good tone, logical fingering. Metronome markings should be regarded as *minimum* speeds. The number of octaves are as given in *Guitar Technique Book* (1999).

KEYS REQUIRED IN GRADE ONE

	New Keys	Review Keys
Major	C, G	None
Minor	a, e	None

SCALES
To be played from memory, ascending AND descending, in the keys stated.
Scale fingerings: Right hand, fingered i-m, using rest or free stroke at the candidate's choice.

	Keys	*M.M.* ♩=	*Articulation*
Major	C, G	92	In quarter notes
Melodic minor	a, e	92	In quarter notes
Harmonic minor	a, e	92	In quarter notes
Chromatic	beginning on D	92	In quarter notes

Note: Do NOT repeat the upper tonic note.
         Do NOT play either the tonic chord or a cadence at the end of the scale.

TRIADS
To be played ascending AND descending in the keys stated.

	Keys	*Position*	*M.M.* $\downarrow$ =	*Note Values*
Broken Triads (Major & Minor)	C, G a, e	Root & Inversions Root & Inversions	92 92	in quarter notes in quarter notes

HARMONIZATION
Candidates are required to play the tonic chord, root position only, in the keys of

Major	C, G
Minor	a, e

Use four-voice texture; open or closed voicing

Example

Sight Reading
Candidates are required to perform at sight a) a rhythmic exercise and b) a passage of guitar score as described below. The candidate will be given a brief period to scan the score, but not to "practise silently" before beginning to play. Candidates must perform each section without counting aloud. It is recommended that candidates maintain a steady beat, and avoid the unnecessary repetition caused by attempting to correct errors during the performance.

a) Rhythm		*b) Guitar Passage*	
To tap, clap or play on one note (at the candidate's choice) a simple rhythm.		To play at sight a simple melody.	
Length	4 bars	Keys	C Major
Time signature	2/4, 3/4	Length	4 bars
Note values	1/2, dotted 1/2, 1/4, 1/8	Time signature	2/4, 3/4, 4/4
Rest values	no rest values	Note values	1/2, dotted 1/2, 1/4
		Rest values	whole rests

Example: a) Rhythm

Example: b) Guitar Passage

Aural Tests

The candidate will be required:

i)   to clap back the rhythmic pattern of a short melody, 4 bars in length, in 2/4 or 3/4 time, consisting of half, dotted half, quarter and eighth notes, after it has been played twice by the Examiner on the guitar or piano. Following is the approximate level of difficulty:

ii) to identify *major* or *minor* triad chords played once by the Examiner in broken form; in close, root position:

iii) the *major* common [four-note] chord of any key will be played once by the Examiner in broken form slowly, ascending and descending. The chord will be in root position. One of the four notes will then be re-sounded for the candidate to identify by saying, at the candidate's choice:
    EITHER   its interval number [1, 3, 5, 8],
    OR   its tonic solfeggio name [doh, me, soh, upper doh].

Viva Voce

Candidates must be prepared to give verbal answers to questions on the TWO List pieces selected for the examination. Candidates must ensure that all teaching notes and other written comments are removed from the score before the examination. The questions will include the following elements:

i)   to find and explain all of the signs (including clefs, time signatures, key signatures, accidentals, etc.), articulation markings (legato, staccato, accents, phrase or slur markings, etc.), dynamic and tempo markings, and other musical terms as they may be found in the three selected pieces.

ii) without reference to the score, to give the title, key and composer of the piece.

iii) to explain the meaning of the title of the piece.

Length of the examination: 20 minutes

Examination Fee: Please consult the current examination application form
for the schedule of fees.

Co-requisite   None. There is NO written examination co-requisite for the
awarding of the Grade 2 Practical Certificate.

Requirements & Marking

Requirement	Total Marks
TWO LIST PIECES	
To be performed from memory	
1	14
2	14
ONE STUDY	12
ONE SUPPLEMENTARY PIECE	10
TECHNICAL TESTS	
Scales & Triads	14
Harmonization	4
SIGHT READING	
Rhythm Pattern	3
Guitar Passage	7
AURAL TESTS	10
VIVA VOCE	6
MARKS FOR MEMORY	6
List pieces only (3 marks each)	
TOTAL POSSIBLE MARKS	100

Pieces

Candidates must be prepared to play TWO pieces from the following list, chosen to contrast in style, key, tempo, etc.. Your choice must include TWO different composers. All pieces must be performed from memory.

LIST PIECES

ANONYMOUS
The Student's Repertoire Series, I — Guitar Solo Pub.
Choose ANY ONE of
  Hungarian Dance
  Lullaby
  Sakura
The Renaissance Guitar — Ariel Music
Choose ANY ONE of
  Wilson's Wilde
  Volt

AGUADO, D.
Waltz in C *(Classical Guitar Technique, I)* — Colombo

CARCASSI, M.
Twenty Selected Waltzes — Reiflinger
Choose ANY ONE of
  Nos. 1, 4

CARULLI, F.
Carulli/Brevier, I — Schott (GA)
Choose ANY ONE of
  Nos. 6, 7, 9, 19
No. 1 of *(Ventiquattro preludi, Op. 114)* — Zerboni
No. 7 of *(18 Piccoli Pezzi, Op. 211)* — Berben

DOMINO & BARTHOLOMEW
I'm Walkin' *(Concepts)* — Big 3 Music

GAGNON, C.
Adagio in A — Doberman
(La guitar Enchantée: pièces facile, I)

GIULIANI, M.
12 Ecossaise Op. 33 — Zerboni
Choose ANY ONE of
  Nos. 1, 8, 9
Andantino *(First Studies Op. 50, No. 10)* — Universal

JACKMAN, R.
Chanson populaire — Doberman
(La guitar Enchantée: pièces très facile, I)

KOSHKIN, N.
Mascarades for Guitar — Lemoine Music
Choose ANY ONE of
  Hopscotch
  The Paper Dragon

MONTREUIL, G.
Divertissements — Doberman
Choose ANY ONE of
  No. 2 Bahamas
  No. 4 Tango pour Mario
  No. 11 Congo

RAK, S.
15 Descriptive Pieces for Guitar — Elderslie Music
Choose ANY ONE of
  An Old Story
  Heavy Sky
  Lullaby
  Storm
  The Sun is Back Again

SANZ, G.
(Instruccion de Musica
Sobre la Guitarra Española, I) — Union Musical
Choose ANY ONE of
  Batalla
  Espanol

SAVIO, I
Maracatu *(Ten Brazilian Folk Tunes)* — Colombo

TANSMAN, A.
12 pieces faciles — Eschig
Choose ANY ONE of
  Vol. I, No. 1, 5
  Vol. II, No. 3

Studies

Candidates must be prepared to play ONE Study chosen from the following list. Memorization is recommended though NOT required.

STUDY LIST

AGUADO, D.
Studi per Chitarra — Zerboni
Choose ANY ONE of
  Nos. 4, 5, 6, 8, 14
8 Lessons for Guitar: — Columbia
  No. 3

BENEDICT, R.
20 Fantasy Etudes, I — Caveat
Choose ANY ONE of
  Nos. 1, 3

BROUWER, L.
Etudes Simples — Eschig
Choose ANY ONE of
  Nos. 2, 4

CARULLI, F.
Studi per Chitarra — Zerboni
Choose ANY ONE of
  Nos. 1, 3, 4

GIULIANI, M.
Studi per Chitarra, Op. 30 — Zerboni
Choose ANY ONE of
  Nos. 9, 10, 15, 21, 27

SAGRERAS, J.
Las Primeras Lecciones — Ricordi
Choose ANY ONE of
  Nos. 53, 54, 65, 67

SOR, F.
Studi per Gitarra — Zerboni
Choose ANY ONE of
  Vol 1, Op. 44, Nos. 9, 11
  Vol. II, Op. 31, No. 1
  Vol. III, Op. 44, Nos. 1, 2,
  Vol. III Op. 60, Nos. 6, 9

Supplementary Piece

Candidates must be prepared to play ONE Supplementary Piece. This piece need not be from the Syllabus lists, and may be chosen entirely at the discretion of the teacher and student. It may represent a period or style of piece not already included in the examination program, but which holds special interest for the candidate. The choice must be within the following guidelines:

1) The equivalent level of difficulty of the piece may be at a higher grade level, providing it is within the technical and musical grasp of the candidate.

2) Pieces below the equivalent of Grade 1 level are not acceptable.

3) The piece must be for solo guitar. Duets and trios are not acceptable.

4) Candidates with exceptional talent for improvisation may wish to improvise upon a theme of their choice. In this case, items 1 and 2 (above) will apply. Marks will be given for originality, musical inventiveness, and structural unity.

Special approval is not required for the Supplementary Piece. However, poor suitability of the choice may be reflected in the mark. Memorization is encouraged, though NOT required.

Technical Tests

Conservatory Canada's booklet *Guitar Technique Book* (1999) contains notational examples for all technical requirements.

All technical tests must be played from memory, evenly, with good tone, logical fingering. Metronome markings should be regarded as *minimum* speeds. The number of octaves are as given in *Guitar Technique Book* (1999).

KEYS REQUIRED IN GRADE TWO

	New Keys	Review Keys
Major	D, F,	G
Minor	b, d,	e

SCALES

To be played from memory, ascending AND descending, in the keys stated.
Scale fingerings: Right hand, fingered i-m, using rest or free stroke at the candidate's choice.

	Keys	*M.M.* $\quad \downarrow =$	*Articulation*
Major	G, D, F	112	In quarter notes
Melodic minor	e, b, d,	112	In quarter notes
Harmonic minor	e, b, d	112	In quarter notes
Chromatic	beginning on A	112	In quarter notes

> Note: Do NOT repeat the upper tonic note.
> Do NOT play either the tonic chord or a cadence at the end of the scale.

TRIADS

To be played ascending AND descending in the keys stated.

	Keys	*Position*	*M.M.* ♩=	*Note Values*
Broken Triads (Major & Minor)	G, D, F e, b, d	Root & Inversions Root & Inversions	104 104	in quarter notes in quarter notes

HARMONIZATION

Candidates are required to play perfect cadences (*i.e.* V-I or i), root position only, in the keys of

Major	D, F
Minor	b, d

Use four-voice texture; open or closed voicing

Example

MAJOR   MINOR

Sight Reading

Candidates are required to perform at sight a) a rhythmic exercise and b) a passage of guitar score as described below. The candidate will be given a brief period to scan the score, but not to "practise silently" before beginning to play. Candidates must perform each section without counting aloud. It is recommended that candidates choose a moderate tempo, maintain a steady beat, and avoid the unnecessary repetition caused by attempting to correct errors during the performance.

a) Rhythm	*b) Guitar Passage*
To tap, clap or play on one note (at the candidate's choice) a simple rhythm. Length — 4 bars Time signature — 3/4, 4/4 Note values — 1/2, dotted 1/2, 1/4, 1/8, & dotted 1/4 followed by 1/8 Rest values — whole, 1/2, 1/4	To play at sight a simple melody. Keys — C, G, F Major Length — 4 bars Time signature — 2/4, 3/4, 4/4 Note values — 1/2, dotted 1/2, 1/4, 1/8 Rest values — whole, 1/2

Example: a) Rhythm

Example: b) Guitar Passage

Aural Tests

The candidate will be required:

i) to clap back the rhythmic pattern of a short melody in 3/4 or 4/4 time, consisting of half, dotted half, quarter, dotted quarter and eighth notes, after it has been played twice by the Examiner on the guitar or piano. Following is the approximate level of difficulty:

ii) to identify *major* or *minor* triad chords played once by the Examiner in broken form and in close, root position.

iii) to identify *major* or *harmonic minor* scales played once by the Examiner, ascending and descending, at a moderately slow tempo.

iv) the *major* common [four-note] chord of any key will be played once by the Examiner in broken form slowly, ascending and descending. The chord will be in root position. One of the four notes will then be re-sounded for the candidate to identify, by saying, at the candidate's choice:
    EITHER   its interval number [1, 3, 5, 8],
    OR   its tonic sol-fa name [doh, me, soh, upper doh].

Viva Voce

Candidates must be prepared to give verbal answers to questions on the THREE List pieces selected for the examination. Candidates must ensure that all teaching notes and other written comments are removed from the score before the examination. The questions will include the following elements:

i) to find and explain all of the signs (including clefs, time signatures, key signatures, accidentals, etc.), articulation markings (legato, staccato, accents, phrase or slur markings, etc.), dynamic and tempo markings, and other musical terms as they may be found in the three selected pieces.

ii) without reference to the score, to give the title, key and composer of the piece.

iii) to explain the meaning of the title of the piece.

___

GRADE THREE

Length of the examination: 20 minutes

Examination Fee: Please consult the current examination application form
for the schedule of fees.

Co-requisite: None. There is NO written examination co-requisite for the
awarding of the Grade 3 Practical Certificate.

Requirements & Marking

Requirement	Total Marks
TWO LIST PIECES	
To be performed from memory	
1	14
2	14
ONE STUDY	12
ONE SUPPLEMENTARY PIECE	10
TECHNICAL TESTS	
Scales, Triads & Arpeggios	14
Harmonization	4
SIGHT READING	
Rhythm Pattern	3
Guitar Passage	7
AURAL TESTS	10
VIVA VOCE	6
MARKS FOR MEMORY	6
List pieces only (2 marks each)	
TOTAL POSSIBLE MARKS	100

Pieces

Candidates must be prepared to play TWO pieces from the following list, chosen to contrast in style, key, tempo, etc.. Your choice must include TWO different composers. All pieces must be performed from memory.

GRADE 3

LIST PIECES

ANONYMOUS
The Student's Repertoire Series   Guitar Solo Pub
Choose ANY ONE of
    Greensleeves
    Irish Dance
Spagnoletta *(The Renaissance Guitar)*   Ariel Music
BACH, J.S./ANZAGHI
Minuetto *(Suite for Keyboard, BWV 822)*   Ricordi
BARNES, M.
Seven Easy Pieces for Solo Guitar   Columbia
Choose ANY ONE of
    Prelude
    March
    Song
BESARD, J.B.
Branle Gay *(The Renaissance Guitar)*   Ariel Music
CARCASSI, M.
Twenty Selected Waltzes   Reiflinger
Choose ANY ONE of
    Nos. 3, 4, 5
CARULLI, F.
18 Piccoli Pezzi, Op. 211   Berben
Choose ANY ONE of
    Nos. 5, 6
Venti-quattro Preludi, Op. 114   Zerboni
Choose ANY ONE of
    Nos. 3, 5
Carulli-Brevier, I   Schott (GA)
Choose ANY ONE of
    Nos. 10, 20
Carulli-Brevier, II   Schott (GA)
Choose ANY ONE of
    Nos. 35, 48
CUTTING, F.
Toy *(The Renaissance Guitar)*   Ariel Music
DOWLAND, J
Orlando Sleepeth *(Four Easy Pieces)*   Universal
ELLINGTON, D.
Jam Blues *(Concepts)*   Big 3 Music
KOSHKIN, N.
Waltz *(Mascarades for Guitar)*   Lemoine Music
LAI, F.
Zoom *(Concepts)*   Big 3 Music
LE ROY, A.
Branle de Bourgogne   Ariel Music
(The Renaissance Guitar)
LOGY, J.A.
Partitia in C Major   Universal
Choose ANY ONE of
    Minuet
    Gigue
Partita in A minor   Universal
Choose ANY ONE of
    Aria
    Capriccio

Sarabande
MONTREUIL, G.
Divertissements, Vol. II   Doberman
Choose ANY ONE of
    Sao Paolo
    Paccale
    Dolores
MOZART, W.A.
Andante Grazioso, K.331   Guitar Solo Pub.
(The Student Repertoire Series)
PAGANINI, N.
Guitar Music Selections   Zimmerman
Choose ANY ONE of
    Nos. 4, 5, 6, 15
RAK, S
15 Descriptive Pieces for Guitar   Elderslie Music
Choose ANY ONE of
    After the Sunset
    Blue Blues
    Country Dance
    Sweet Song
    The Daybreak
    The Storm is Over
SANZ, G.
Instruccion de Musica:
Sobra la Guitarra Española   Union Musical
Choose ANY ONE of
    Libro I, No. I Gallardo
    Libro II, No. 54 Canciones
    Gallardas   Eschig
(Les Guitaristes espagñol du XVIIe siecle)
SAVIO, I
Ten Brazilian Folk Tunes   Colombo
Choose ANY ONE of
    Maracatu
    Modinha
    Samba Lelé
SOR, F.
First Studies, Op. 31   Universal
Choose ANY ONE of
    Nos. 3, 16, 17
TANSMAN, A.
12 Pieces Faciles   Eschig
Choose ANY ONE of
    Vol I: Nos. 10, 11
    Vol. II: *Nos. 9, 10*
TOROK, A.
Sketches from Life   Waterloo Music
Play ANY ONE of
    Aimée
    A Sad Journey
    So Mad
TRADITIONAL
Old Time Religion *(Concepts)*   Big 3 Music

Studies

Candidates must be prepared to play ONE Study chosen from the following list.   Memorization is recommend though NOT required.

GRADE 3

STUDY LIST

AGUADO, D.
Studi per Chitarra — Zerboni
  Choose ANY ONE of
    Nos. 16, 18, 20, 22, 26
8 Lessons for Guitar — Columbia
  Choose ANY ONE of
    Nos. 6, 7

BENEDICT, R.
Twenty Fantasy Etudes, I — Caveat
  Choose ANY ONE of
    Nos. 2, 4, 5

BROUWER, L.
Etude Simples — Eschig
  No. 1

CARCASSI, M.
First Studies — Universal
  No. 4 Allegretto

GIULIANI, M.
Studi Per Chitarra — Zerboni
  Choose ANY ONE of
    Op. 30, Nos. 16, 19, 22, 31
    Op. 51, Nos. 3, 12

SAGRERAS, J.
Las Primeras Lecciones — Ricordi
  Choose ANY ONE of
    Nos. 67, 80, 82, 83, 84, 85

SOR, F.
Studi per chitarra Op. 44 Vol. I — Zerboni
  Choose ANY ONE of
    Nos. 5, 8

Supplementary Piece

Candidates must be prepared to play ONE Supplementary Piece. This piece need not be from the Syllabus lists, and may be chosen entirely at the discretion of the teacher and student. It may represent a period or style of piece not already included in the examination program, but which holds special interest for the candidate. The choice must be within the following guidelines:

1) The equivalent level of difficulty of the piece may be at a higher grade level, providing it is within the technical and musical grasp of the candidate.

2) Pieces below the equivalent of Grade 2 level of difficulty are not acceptable.

3) The piece must be for solo guitar. Duets and trios are not acceptable.

4) Candidates with exceptional talent for improvisation may wish to improvise upon a theme of their choice. In this case, items 1 and 2 (above) will apply. Marks will be given for originality, musical inventiveness, and structural unity.

Special approval is not required for the Supplementary Piece. However, poor suitability of the choice may be reflected in the mark. Memorization is encouraged, though NOT required.

Technical Tests

Conservatory Canada's booklet *Guitar Technique Book* (1999) contains notational examples for all technical requirements.

All technical tests must be played from memory, evenly, with good tone, logical fingering. Metronome markings should be regarded as *minimum* speeds. The number of octaves are as given in *Guitar Technique Book* (1999).

KEYS REQUIRED IN GRADE THREE

	New Keys	Review Keys
Major	A, B♭	D
Minor	f♯, g	b

SCALES

To be played from memory, ascending AND descending, in the keys stated.

Scale fingerings: Right hand, fingered i-m or m-a (to be specified by the examiner), using rest or free stroke at the candidate's choice.

	Keys	*M.M.* ♩=	*Articulation*
Major	D, A, B♭	120	In quarter notes
Melodic minor	b, f♯, g	120	In quarter notes
Harmonic minor	b, f♯, g	120	In quarter notes
Chromatic	beginning on E	120	In quarter notes

Note: Do NOT repeat the upper tonic note.
Do NOT play either the tonic chord or a cadence at the end of the scale.

TRIADS

To be played ascending AND descending in the keys stated.

	Keys	*Position*	*M.M.* ♩=	*Note Values*
Solid Triads (Major & Minor)	A, B♭ f♯, g	Root & Inversions	50	in quarter notes, each position separated by a quarter rest.

ARPEGGIOS

To be played ascending AND descending in the keys stated.

	Keys	*Position*	*M.M.* ♩=	*Note Values*
Major	B♭	Root only	60	in eighth notes
Minor	g	Root only	60	in eighth notes

HARMONIZATION

Candidates are required to play Plagal cadences (i.e. IV-I or iv-i), root position only, in the keys of

14

Major	A, B♭
Minor	g, f♯

Use four-voice texture; open or closed voicing

Example

Sight Reading

Candidates are required to perform at sight a) a rhythmic exercise and b) a passage of guitar score as described below. The candidate will be given a brief period to scan the score, but not to "practise silently" before beginning to play. Candidates must perform each section without counting aloud. It is recommended that candidates maintain a steady beat, and avoid the unnecessary repetition caused by attempting to correct errors during the performance.

a) Rhythm		b) Guitar Passage	
To tap or play on one note (at the candidate's choice) a simple rhythm.		To play at sight a simple melody.	
Length	4 bars	Keys	C, G, F Major & a minor
Time signature	2/4, 3/4, 4/4	Length	4-8 bars
Note values	whole,1/2, dotted 1/2, 1/4, 1/8	Time signature	2/4, 3/4, 4/4
	& dotted 1/4 followed by 1/8	Note values	whole, 1/2, dotted 1/2, 1/4, 1/8
Rest values	whole, 1/2, 1/4, 1/8	Rest values	whole, 1/2, 1/4

Example: a) Rhythm

Example: b) Guitar Passage

Aural Tests

The candidate will be required:

i)   to clap back the rhythmic pattern of a short melody in 2/4, 3/4 or 4/4 time, consisting of whole, half, dotted half, quarter, dotted quarter and eighth notes, after it has been played twice by the Examiner on the guitar or piano. Following is the approximate level of difficulty:

ii)   to identify *major* or *minor* triad chords played once by the Examiner in solid form and in close, root position.

iii)   to identify *major or harmonic minor* or *melodic minor* scales played once by the Examiner, ascending and descending, at a moderate tempo.

iv)   the *major* **or** *minor* common [four-note] chord of any key will be played once by the Examiner in broken form slowly, ascending and descending. The chord will be in root position. One of the four notes will then be re-sounded for the candidate to identify, by saying, at the candidate's choice:

        EITHER   (1) its interval number [1, 3, 5, 8],
        OR   (2) its tonic sol-fa name.

Viva Voce

Candidates must be prepared to give verbal answers to questions on the THREE List pieces selected for the examination. Candidates must ensure that all teaching notes and other written comments are removed from the score before the examination. The questions will include the following elements:

i)   to find and explain all of the signs (including clefs, time signatures, key signatures, accidentals, etc.), articulation markings (legato, staccato, accents, phrase or slur markings, etc.), dynamic and tempo markings, and other musical terms as they may be found in the three selected pieces.

ii)   without reference to the score, to give the title, key and composer of the piece.

iii)   to explain the meaning of the title of the piece.

GRADE FOUR

Length of the examination: 25 minutes

Examination Fee: Please consult the current examination application form for the schedule of fees.

Co-requisite: None. There is NO written examination co-requisite for the awarding of the Grade 4 Practical Certificate.

Requirements & Marking

Requirement	Total Marks
THREE LIST PIECES To be performed from memory List A 1	12
List B 1	10
2	10
ONE STUDY	9
ONE SUPPLEMENTARY PIECE	7
TECHNICAL TESTS Scales, Triads, Arpeggios	14
Harmonization	4
SIGHT READING Rhythm Pattern	3
Guitar Passage	7
AURAL TESTS	10
VIVA VOCE	8
MARKS FOR MEMORY List pieces only (2 marks each)	6
TOTAL POSSIBLE MARKS	100

Pieces

Candidates must be prepared to play THREE pieces, one from *List A* and two from *List B*, chosen to contrast in style, key, tempo, etc.. Your choice must include THREE different composers. All pieces must be performed from memory.

GRADE 4

LIST A

ATTAIGNANT, P.
Basse Dance *(Guitar Solos from France)*   Biberian

BESSARD, J.B.
Courante *(Guitar Solos from France)*   Biberian

CORBETTA, F.
Les Guitaristes Italiens du XVIIeme Siecle   Eschig
Choose ANY ONE of
     Le Tombeau Sur La Mort de Madame L'Orléans
     Passacaille

DOWLAND, J.
Nine Pieces (Duarte)   Universal
Choose ANY ONE of
     Mrs. Winter's Jump
     Mrs. Nichol's Allemande
     English Dance

LOGY, J.A.
Partita in A minor   Universal
Choose ANY ONE of
     Gavotte
     Gigue

PISADOR, D.
Villanesca   Eschig
(Les Guitaristes Espagñol du XVIeme Siecle)

SANZ, G.
*Instruccion de Musica Sobre
la Guitarra Española*   Real
Choose ANY ONE of
     No. 25 Danza de La Hachas
     No. 31 Rugers Y Paradetas
     No. 32 Matachin

LIST B

BENEDICT, R.
Twenty Fantasy Etudes, I   Caveat
Choose ANY ONE of
     Fantasy 2, 5

CARCASSI, M.
Caprice No. 3 *(Six Caprices Op. 26)*   Schwarz

CARULLI, F.
Carulli-Brevier Vol. II: Scott
Choose ANY ONE of
     Nos. 45, 46, 50

GAGNON, C.
Cornemuse *(La guitar Enchantée)*   Doberman

GIULIANI, M.
Divertimenti Op. 40:   Schott (GA)
Choose ANY ONE of
     Nos. 3, 11
Complete Works, Vol. 8   Halstan
Choose ANY ONE of
     Bagatelles Nos. 2, 7

GUERAU, F.
Les Guitaristes Espagñols du XVIIeme Siecle   Eschig
Choose ANY ONE of
     Españoleta
     Air de danse

KOSHKIN, N.
Mascarades for Guitar   Lemoine Music
Choose ANY ONE of
     Pulcineloa
     Reflections of the Moon

LATOUCHE, FETTER & DUKE
Taking a Chance on Love *(Concepts)*   Big 3 Music

LEWIS & KLENNER
Just Friends *(Concepts)*   Big 3 Music

PAGANINI, N.
36 Stucke, I   Zimmerman
Choose ANY ONE of
     No. 2, 3, 15, 17

PREVIN, D. & A.
The Fortune Cookie *(Concepts)*   Big 3 Music

RAK, S.
15 Descriptive Pieces for Guitar   Elderslie Music
Choose ANY ONE of
     On the Ocean
     The Old Castle

RIERA, R.
Nostalgia *(Four Venezuelan Pieces)*   Universal

SCHONBERGER, C. & E.
Whispering *(Concepts)*   Big 3 Music

SOR, F.
Andante, Op. 47, No. 1 *(Guitar Works, VI)*   Tecla
Studi per Chitarra, III   Zerboni
Choose ANY ONE of
     Op. 44, Nos. 21, 22

TANSMAN, A.
12 Pieces Faciles   Eschig
Choose ANY ONE of
     Vol. I, No. 7 Tarantella
     Vol. I, No. 9 Toccata
     Vol. II, No. 11 A l'espagnol

TOROK, A.
Sketches of Life   Waterloo
Choose ANY ONE of
     Blue Shuffle
     Chorale
     Dooda
     Dream
     Fond Memory

WEINZWEIG, J.
18 Pieces for Guitar   Columbia
Choose ANY ONE of
     No. 2 Glissado
     No. 3 Promenade

TRADITIONAL
Concepts   Big 3 Music
Choose ANY ONE of
     Bold MacDonald
     Bonnie
     Greensleeves part one
     My Grandfather's Clock
     St. James Infirmary

Studies

Candidates must be prepared to play ONE Study chosen from the following List. Memorization is recommended though NOT required.

STUDY LIST

AGUADO, D.
Studi per Chitarra   Zerboni
  Choose ANY ONE of
    Nos. 10, 17, 25, 27

BROUWER, L.
Etudes Simples   Eschig
  Choose ANY ONE of
    No. 5, 6, 7

CARCASSI, M.
25 Melodious Progressive Studies, Op. 60   Fisher
  No. 6

CARULLI, F.
Studi per Chitarra   Zerboni
  Choose ANY ONE of
    No. 14, 20, 27

Op. 100   Zerboni
  Choose ANY ONE of
    Nos. 11, 12, 13

Op. 139   Zerboni
  Choose ANY ONE of
    Nos. 4, 6, 11

GIULIANI, M.
Oeuvres Choisies pour Guitare, Op. 1   Heugel
  Choose ANY ONE of
    Nos. 6, 8

SAGRERAS, J.
Las Segundas Lecciones   Chanterelle
  Choose ANY ONE of
    Nos. 6, 7, 11, 16

SOR, F./SEGOVIA
Twenty Studies for the Guitar   Marks Music
  Choose ANY ONE of
    Nos. 2, 3, 4

TÁRREGA, F.
Etude No. I *(Etuden)*   Universal

Supplementary Piece

Candidates must be prepared to play ONE Supplementary Piece. This piece need not be from the Syllabus lists, and may be chosen entirely at the discretion of the teacher and student. It may represent a period or style of piece not already included in the examination program, but which holds special interest for the candidate. The choice must be within the following guidelines:

1) The equivalent level of difficulty of the piece may be at a higher grade level, providing it is within the technical and musical grasp of the candidate.

2) Pieces below the equivalent of Grade 3 level of difficulty are not acceptable.

3) The piece must be for solo guitar. Duets and trios are not acceptable.

4) Candidates with exceptional talent for improvisation may wish to improvise upon a theme of their choice. In this case, items 1 and 2 (above) will apply. Marks will be given for originality, musical inventiveness, and structural unity.

Special approval is not required for the Supplementary Piece. However, poor suitability of the choice may be reflected in the mark. Memorization is encouraged, though NOT required.

Technical Tests

Conservatory Canada's booklet *Guitar Technique Book* (1999) contains notational examples for all technical requirements.

All technical tests must be played from memory, evenly, with good tone, logical fingering. Metronome markings should be regarded as *minimum* speeds. The number of octaves are as given in ***Guitar Technique Book*** (1999).

KEYS REQUIRED IN GRADE FOUR

	New Keys	Review Keys
Major	E, E$^\flat$	D, A
Minor	c$^\sharp$, c	f$^\sharp$

SCALES
To be played from memory, ascending AND descending, in the keys stated.

Scale fingerings: Right hand, fingered i-m, m-a, or i-a (to be specified by the examiner), using rest or free stroke at the candidate's choice.

	Keys	M.M. $\downarrow$ =	Articulation
Major	A, E, E$^\flat$	72	In eighth notes
Melodic minor	f$^\sharp$, c$^\sharp$, c	72	In eighth notes
Harmonic minor	f$^\sharp$, c$^\sharp$, c	72	In eighth notes
Chromatic	beginning on A	72	In eighth notes
Slur	D, A	52	In eighth notes

Note: Do NOT repeat the upper tonic note.
        Do NOT play either the tonic chord or a cadence at the end of the scale.

TRIADS
To be played ascending AND descending in the keys stated.

	Keys	Position	M.M. $\downarrow$ =	Note Values
Solid Triads (Major & Minor)	E, E$^\flat$ c, c$^\sharp$	Root & Inversions	60	in quarter notes, each position separated by a quarter rest.

ARPEGGIOS
To be played ascending AND descending in the keys stated.

	Keys	Position	M.M. $\downarrow$ =	Note Values
Major	E, E$^\flat$	Root only	66	in eighth notes
Minor	c, c$^\sharp$	Root only	66	in eighth notes

HARMONIZATION

Candidates are required to play the chord progression I-IV-V-I and i-iv-V-i, root position only, in the keys of

Major	E, E^b
Minor	c$^\#$, c

Use four-voice texture; open or closed voicing

Example

Sight Reading

Candidates are required to perform at sight a) a rhythmic exercise and b) a passage of guitar score as described below. The candidate will be given a brief period to scan the score, but not to "practise silently" before beginning to play. Candidates must perform each section without counting aloud. It is recommended that candidates maintain a steady beat, and avoid the unnecessary repetition caused by attempting to correct errors during the performance.

a) *Rhythm*	b) *Guitar Passage*
To tap, clap or play on one note (at the candidate's choice) a simple rhythm. Length — 4 bars Time signature — 2/4, 3/4, 4/4 Note values — whole, 1/2, dotted 1/2, 1/4, 1/8, dotted 1/4 followed by 1/8, dotted 1/8 followed by 1/16. Rest values — whole, 1/2, 1/4, 1/8	To play at sight a simple guitar passage. Keys — Major - C, G, D, F, B^b Minor - a, e, d Length — 4-8 bars Time Signature — 2/4, 3/4, 4/4 Note values — whole, 1/2, dotted 1/2, 1/4, 1/8 Rest values — whole, 1/2, 1/4

Example: a) Rhythm

Example: b) Guitar Passage

Aural Tests

The candidate will be required:

21

i) at the candidate's choice, to play back OR sing back to any vowel, a short melody of six to eight notes, in 2/4, 3/4 or 4/4 time, based on the first five notes of a major scale, after the Examiner has:

       ✓ named the key [only the major keys of *C, F, G* or *D* will be used]

       ✓ played the 4-note chord on the tonic in broken form

       ✓ played the melody twice

The melody will begin on the tonic note. Following is the approximate level of difficulty:

ii) to identify any of the following intervals after each one has been played once by the Examiner in broken form:

ABOVE a given note	**BELOW a note**
major 3rd	*perfect 4th*
minor 3rd	*perfect 5th*
perfect 4th	*perfect octave*
perfect 5th	
perfect octave	

iii) to identify *major* or *minor* triad chords, solid form, in close, root position only. Each triad chord will be played ONCE by the examiner.

iv) to state whether a short passage in *chorale* style, about 6 to 8 bars in length, is in a *major* or a *minor* key, and whether the final cadence is either ***Perfect*** (V-I) or ***Interrupted/Deceptive*** (V-VI).

Viva Voce

Candidates must be prepared to give verbal answers to questions on the THREE List pieces selected for the examination. Candidates must ensure that all teaching notes and other written comments are removed from the score before the examination. The questions will include the following elements:

i) to find and explain all of the signs (including clefs, time signatures, key signatures, accidentals, etc.), articulation markings (legato, staccato, accents, phrase or slur markings, etc.), dynamic and tempo markings, and other musical terms as they may be found in the three selected pieces.

ii) without reference to the score, to give the title, key and composer of the piece.

iii) to explain the meaning of the title of the piece.

iv) to give a few relevant details about the composer.

v) with direct reference to the score, to explain briefly simple form and key structures, including any obvious modulations.

GRADE FIVE

Length of the examination: 25 minutes

Examination Fee: Please consult the current examination application form for the schedule of fees.

Co-requisite: Successful completion of the following written examination is required for the awarding of the Grade 5 Practical Certificate.
Theory 1

Requirements & Marking

Requirement	Total Marks
THREE LIST PIECES To be performed from memory List A 1	12
List B 1	10
2	10
ONE STUDY	9
ONE SUPPLEMENTARY PIECE	7
TECHNICAL TESTS Scales, Triads, Arpeggios	14
Harmonization	4
SIGHT READING Rhythm Pattern	3
Guitar Passage	7
AURAL TESTS	10
VIVA VOCE (List Pieces only)	8
MARKS FOR MEMORY List pieces only (2 marks each)	6
TOTAL POSSIBLE MARKS	100

Pieces

Candidates must be prepared to play THREE pieces, one from *List A* and two from *List B*, chosen to contrast in style, key, tempo, etc.. Your choice must include THREE different composers. All pieces must be performed from memory.

LIST A

ANONYMOUS
The Maid in Constrite   Oxford
   (Three Pieces from...Pickering Lute Book)
Six Lute Pieces of the Renaissance   Columbia
   Choose ANY ONE of
    Nos. 1, 2, 3, 4
ATTAIGNANT, P.
Branle Gay *(Guitar Solos from France)*   Biberian
BALLARDE, R.
Ballet Des Mamans   Biberian
   (Guitar Solos from France)
DE VISEE, R./CHIESA
Suite in D Minor   Universal
   Choose ANY ONE of
    Minuet
    Courante
DOWLAND, J.
Seven Pieces (Poulton)   Schott (GA)
   Choose ANY ONE of
    Mrs. White's Nothing
    Dowland's Bells
    Galliard
    K. Darcie's Spirit
    My Lady Hunsdon's Puffe
The Round Battle Galliard   Ariel Music
   (The Renaissance Guitar)
GERRITS, P.
Prelude *(Music for Solo Guitar, I)*   Doberman
LOGY, J.A.
Partita in C   Universal
   Choose ANY TWO of
    Courante
    Sarabande
    Gavotte
MILAN, L.
Pavan I *(El Maestro)*   Union Musical
MUDARRA, A.
Romanesca II   Union Musical
PURCELL, H./BREAM
Hornpipe *(Four Pieces)*   Faber
A New Irish Tune *(Album of Guitar Solos)*   Columbia
ROBINSON, T.
Walking in a Country Town *(Five Pieces)*   Schott
SANZ, G.
Chaconna *(Instruccion de Musica: sobra*   Union Musical
   la Guitarra Española)
Spanish Suite   Waterloo
   Choose ANY ONE of
    II Villano
    IV Españoleta
WEISS, S.L.
Eleven Pieces from the London Manuscripts Ricordi
   Choose ANY ONE of
    Nos. 4, 5

LIST B

ALMEIDA, L.
Contemporary Moods for Classical Guitar   Robbins Music
   Choose ANY ONE of
    Shadow of Your Smile
    Blue Moon
    Mimi
ANONYMOUS
Spanish Romance   Any edition
BAKER, M.
Mickey Baker's Complete
Course in Jazz Guitar, II   Lewis
   Choose ANY ONE of
    Pathos
    Lost Lament
    Just Bobi
BARRIOS, A. MANGORE
Minuet en do *(Guitar Works, I)*   Belwin
BELLAVANCE, G.
Music for Solo Guitar, II   Doberman
   Choose ANY ONE of
    Etude No. 1
    Etude No. 2
BROWN & FAIN
That Old Feeling *(Concepts)*   Big 3 Music
CAMILLERI, C.
Four African Sketches   Cramer
   Choose ANY ONE of
    Nos. 1, 4
CARCASSI, M.
Carcassi/Brevier, II   Schott
   No. 29
CARULLI, F.
Andante, Op. 121, No. 18   Any edition
COSTE, N.
Duex Quadrilles (Guitar Works, IX)   Chanterelle
   Choose ANY ONE of
    Nos. 1, 2, 5
DIABELLI, A.
Sonata in C (3rd Mov't)   Schott
GIULIANI, M.
Divertimenti, Op. 40:   Schott
   Choose ANY ONE of
    Nos. 2, 6, 8, 2
KLAGES & GREER
Just You, Just Me *(Concepts)*   Big 3 Music
LEWIS, YOUNG & HENDERSON
Five Foot Two *(Concepts)*   Big 3 Music
MOLINO, F.
Rondeau No. 3 *(Six Rondeau, Op. 11)*   Schott (GA)
PAGANINI, N.
Sonatine No. 4 *(36 Stucke, II)*   Zimmerman
RIERA, R.
Melancolia *(Four Venezuelan Pieces)*   Universal
TÁRREGA, F.
Lagrima   Any edition
Adelita   Any edition
Prelude No. 10   Any edition
Prelude No. 11   Any edition
TOROK, A.
Sketches from Life   Waterloo
   Choose ANY ONE of
    Signora Pulgar
    Bad Weather
    Goodbye
    Sahara Trills
    T.V. Madness
    So Many Regrets

Studies

Candidates must be prepared to play ONE Study chosen from the following List.   Memorization is recommended though NOT required.

STUDY LIST

AGUADO, D.
Studi per Chitarra   Zerboni
  Choose ANY ONE of
    Nos. 21, 29, 35, 36, 39
BENEDICT, R.
Etude No. 11 *(Twenty Fantasy Etudes, I)*   Caveat
BROUWER, L.
Etude No. 3 *(Etudes Simples)*   Eschig
COSTE, N.
Etude No. 13 *(25 Etudes, Op. 38)*   Schott (GA)
CARCASSI, M.
25 Melodious & Progressive Studie   C. Fisher
  Choose ANY ONE of
    No. 3, 4, 7, 8, 10, 16
GIULIANI, M.
24 Etudes Op. 48   Schott (GA)
  Choose ANY ONE of
    Nos. 1, 2
Studi Per Chitarra, Op. 30   Zerboni
  No. 26
Studi Per Chitarra, Op. 51   Zerboni
  Choose ANY ONE of
    Nos. 14, 15, 16

Studi Per Chitarra, Op. 48   Zerboni
  No. 15
SAGRERAS, J.
Les Terceras Lecciones   Ricordi
  Choose ANY ONE of
    Nos. 32, 36, 38
Les Cuartas Lecciones   Ricordi
  Choose ANY ONE of
    Nos. 10, 12
SOR, F./CHIESA
Studi per Chitarra, Op. 35, Vol. II   Zerboni
  Choose ANY ONE of
    Nos. 8 to 15
SOR, F./SEGOVIA
Twenty Studies: Marks Music
  Choose ANY ONE of
    Nos. 2, 4, 5
TANSMAN, A.
No. 12 Etude *(12 Pièces Faciles, II)*   Eschig
TÁRREGA, F.
Etuden   Universal
  Choose ANY ONE of
    Nos. 1, 4, 6

Supplementary Piece

Candidates must be prepared to play ONE Supplementary Piece. This piece need not be from the Syllabus lists, and may be chosen entirely at the discretion of the teacher and student. It may represent a period or style of piece not already included in the examination program, but which holds special interest for the candidate. The choice must be within the following guidelines:

1) The equivalent level of difficulty of the piece may be at a higher grade level, providing it is within the technical and musical grasp of the candidate.

2) Pieces below the equivalent of Grade 4 level of difficulty are not acceptable.

3) The piece must be for solo guitar. Duets and trios are not acceptable.

4) Candidates with exceptional talent for improvisation may wish to improvise upon a theme of their choice. In this case, items 1 and 2 (above) will apply. Marks will be given for originality, musical inventiveness, and structural unity.

5) Candidates may choose to play a piece of music from standard real book form chosen either from any "Fake" Book or from *40 Compositions in Standard Real Form*. In this case, items 1 and 2 (above) will apply. Candidates must play both the melody and a suitable accompaniment. Marks will be given for a stylistic performance.

Special approval is not required for the Supplementary Piece. However, poor suitability of the choice may be reflected in the mark. Memorization is encouraged, though NOT required.

Technical Tests

Conservatory Canada's booklet *Guitar Technique Book* (1999) contains notational examples for all technical requirements.

All technical tests must be played from memory, evenly, with good tone, logical fingering. Metronome markings should be regarded as *minimum* speeds. The number of octaves are as given in *Guitar Technique Book* (1999).

KEYS REQUIRED IN GRADE FIVE

	New Keys	**Review Keys**
Major	B, A^b	C, G, E^b
Minor	g$^{\#}$, f	c

SCALES

To be played from memory, ascending AND descending, in the keys stated.

Scale fingerings: Right hand, fingered i-m, m-a, and i-a, using rest and free stroke (to be specified by the examiner), . Use only movable, closed string left-hand fingering (except open 6th string).

	Keys	*M.M.* $\downarrow$ =	*Articulation*
Major	B, E^b, A^b	58	In triplet eighth notes AND sixteenth notes
Melodic minor	g$^{\#}$, c, f	58	In triplet eighth notes AND sixteenth notes
Harmonic minor	g$^{\#}$, c, f	58	In triplet eighth notes AND sixteenth notes
Major: Repeated Notes	B, A^b	66	In triplet eighth notes
Melodic minor: Repeated Notes	g$^{\#}$, f	66	In triplet eighth notes
Slur	C, G	66	In eighth notes
Chromatic	beginning on E	66	In sixteenth notes
Whole Tone	beginning on C	88	In eighth notes

Note: Do NOT repeat the upper tonic note.
Do NOT play either the tonic chord or a cadence at the end of the scale.

TRIADS

To be played ascending AND descending in the keys stated.

	Keys	*Position*	*M.M.* $\downarrow$ =	*Note Values*
Solid Triads (Major & Minor)	B, A^b g$^{\#}$, f	Root & Inversions	72	in quarter notes WITHOUT rests.

ARPEGGIOS

To be played, ascending AND descending, in the keys stated.

	Keys	*Position*	*M.M.* ♩=	*Articulation*
(Major & Minor)	B, A♭ g#, f	root	72	in eighth notes
Dominant 7th	in the KEYS OF B, A♭	root	72	in eighth notes

HARMONIZATION

Candidates are required to play the chord progression I-IV-V-I and i-iv-V-i, root position only, in the keys of

Major	B, A♭
Minor	g#, f

Use four-voice texture; open or closed voicing

Example

MAJOR ... MINOR

I   IV   V   I   i   iv   V   i

Sight Reading

Candidates are required to perform at sight a) a rhythmic exercise and b) a passage of guitar score as described below. The candidate will be given a brief period to scan the score, but not to "practise silently" before beginning to play. Candidates must perform each section without counting aloud. It is recommended that candidates maintain a steady beat, and avoid the unnecessary repetition caused by attempting to correct errors during the performance.

a) Rhythm	*b) Guitar Passage*
To tap, clap or play on one note (at the candidate's choice) a simple rhythm.	To play at sight a short guitar piece about equal in difficulty to pieces of Grade 2 level.
Length 4 bars	Keys Major & Minor up to and including 2 sharps or flats.
Time signature 2/4, 3/4, 4/4	
Note values variety of values including triplets and ties	Length 8-12 bars
Rest values whole, 1/2, 1/4, 1/8	

Example: a) Rhythm

Aural Tests

The candidate will be required:

i)   at the candidate's choice, to play back OR sing back to any vowel, a short melody of six to eight notes, in 2/4, 3/4 or 4/4 time, based on the first five notes and the lower leading tone of a *major* scale, after the Examiner has:
✓ named the key [only the major keys of *C, F, G* or *D* will be used]
✓ played the 4-note chord on the tonic in broken form
✓ played the melody twice.

The melody will begin on the tonic note. Following is the approximate level of difficulty:

ii)   to identify any of the following intervals after the Examiner has played each one once in broken form:

ABOVE a note	BELOW a note
major 3rd	*major 3rd*
minor 3rd	*minor 3rd*
perfect 4th	*perfect 4th*
perfect 5th	*perfect 5th*
major 6th	*perfect octave*
minor 6th	
perfect octave	

iii)   to identify *major* or *minor* triads and *dominant 7th* chords, solid form, in close, root position only. Each triad/chord will be played ONCE by the Examiner.

iv)   to state whether a short piece in *chorale* style is in a *major* or a *minor* key, and whether the final cadence is ***Perfect*** (V-I) or ***Plagal*** (IV-I).

Viva Voce

Candidates must be prepared to give verbal answers to questions on the THREE List pieces selected for the examination. Candidates must ensure that all teaching notes and other written comments are removed from the score before the examination. The questions will include the following elements:

i)   to find and explain all of the signs (including clefs, time signatures, key signatures, accidentals, etc.), articulation markings (legato, staccato, accents, phrase or slur markings, etc.), dynamic and tempo markings, and other musical terms as they may be found in the three selected pieces.

ii)   without reference to the score, to give the title, key and composer of the piece.

iii) to explain the meaning of the title of the piece.

iv)   to give a few relevant details about the composer (List A and List B only).

v)   with direct reference to the score, to explain briefly simple form and key structures, including any obvious modulations.

GRADE SIX

Length of the examination: 30 minutes

Examination Fee: Please consult the current examination application form
for the schedule of fees.

Co-requisite: Successful completion of the following written examination is
required for the awarding of the Grade 6 Practical Certificate.
Theory 2

Requirements & Marking

Requirement	Total Marks
THREE LIST PIECES	
To be performed from memory, one from each of	
List A	11
List B	11
List C	11
ONE STUDY	9
ONE SUPPLEMENTARY PIECE	8
TECHNICAL TESTS	
Scales, Triads, Arpeggios	14
Harmonization	4
SIGHT READING	2
Rhythm Pattern	6
Guitar Passage	
AURAL TESTS	8
VIVA VOCE (List Pieces only)	6
MARKS FOR MEMORY (2 marks each)	6
TOTAL POSSIBLE MARKS	100

Pieces

Candidates must be prepared to play THREE pieces, one from *List A*, *List B* and *List C*, chosen to
contrast in style, key, tempo, etc.. Your choice must include THREE different composers. All pieces
must be performed from memory.

GRADE 6

LIST A

ANONYMOUS
    The Cobbler *(The Renaissance Guitar)*   Ariel Music
BACH, J.S.
    Bourrée *(Lute Suite, BWV 996)*   Any edition
BRESCIANELLO, G.A.
    Partita in E minor: Waterloo
    Choose ANY MOVEMENT
CABEZON, A. DE
    Hymno a trés *(Tre composizioni)*   Zerboni
DE VISEE, R./VAN FEGGLEN
    Suite in D minor   Berben
        Allemande
        Gigue
DOWLAND, J.
    King of Denmark's Galliard   Any Edition
    Tarlton's Resurrection   Ariel Music
    (The Renaissance Guitar)
JOHNSON, R.
    Alman *(The Renaissance Guitar)*   Ariel Music
MERTEL, E.
    Ballet *(The Renaissance Guitar)*   Ariel Music
MILAN, L.
    Fantasia Del Quarto Tona   Schott
    Choose ANY ONE of
        Nos. 2, 4
PURCELL, H.
    Air and Minuet *(Four Pieces)*   Faber
    Jig *(Album of Guitar Solos)*   Columbia
WEISS, S.L.
    Eleven Pieces from the London Manuscripts Ricordi
    Choose ANY ONE of
        No. 2 Minuet
        No. 3 Bouree
        No. 10 Rigardon

LIST B

BARRIOS MANGORE, A.
    Guitar Works   Belwin
    Choose ANY ONE of
        Mabelita
        Madrecita
CARULLI, F.
    Rondo, Op. 241, No. 10   Any edition
COSTE, N.
    Guitar Works, IX   Chanterelle
    Choose ANY ONE of
        Andantino
        Pastorale
        Valse in A
DIABELLI, A.
    Sonata in C (4th mov't)   Schott
GIULIANI, M.
    Divertimenti, Op. 40   Schott
    Choose ANY ONE of
        Nos. 4, 7
GLUCK, C. W./SEGOVIA
    Ballet *(Album of Guitar Solos)*   Colomba
GREIG, E.
    Valse, Op. 12, No. 2 *(Classical Montage)*   Waterloo

MOLINO, F.
    Six Rondeaux, Op. 11   Schott (GA)
    Choose ANY ONE of
        Nos. 4, 5
PONCE, M.
    Cancion No. 1 *(Tres Cancione populaire)*   Schott
    Préludes, I   Schott
    Play both Nos. 5 AND 6
SOR, F.
    Andantino, Op. 2 No. 3   Any edition
    Minuet in C *(Grande Sonate, Op. 22)*   Any edition
    Minuet in C *(Grande Sonate, Op. 25)*   Any edition
TANSMAN, A.
    Suite in modo polonica   Eschig
    Choose ANY ONE of
        Nos. 1, 2, 3, 4, 5, 6
TÁRREGA, F.
    Prelude I   Ricordi
    Prelude V   Ricordi

LIST C

ALMEIDA, L.
    Contemporary Moods for Classical Guitar   Robbins Music
    Choose ANY ONE of
        Over the Rainbow
        Mam'selle
        The Green Fields of Summer
BALADA, L./LIMA
    Lento *(Suite No. 1, Lima)*   Colombo
BENEDICT, R.
    Divertimenti: No. 1   Waterloo
CAMILLERI, C.
    Four African Sketches   Cramer
    Choose ANY ONE of
        Nos. 2, 3
CARLEVARO, A.
    Rondo *(Preludios Americanos)*   Barry-Buenos
    Aires
COTE, R.
    Melody Lyrique   Waterloo
KOSHKIN, N.
    Mascarades for Guitar   Lemoine Music
    Choose ANY ONE of
        Pastorale
        Gnomes in the Grass
LAURO, A.
    Registro *(Suite Venezolana)*   Brock
TOROK, A.
    Sketches from Life   Waterloo
    Choose ANY ONE of
        March
        Primavera
        Landauer's Bells
WEINZWEG, J.
    18 Pieces for Guitar   CMC
    Choose ANY ONE of
        Meditation
        Oscillation

GRADE 6

Studies

Candidates must be prepared to play ONE Study chosen from the following List. Memorization is recommended though NOT required.

STUDY LIST

AGUADO, D
Studi per Chitarra — Zerboni
Choose ANY ONE of
Nos. 37, 42

BROUWER, L.
Etudes Simples — Eschig
No. 8

CARCASSI, M.
25 Melodious Studies, Op. 60 — Fisher
Choose ANY ONE of
Nos. 9, 12, 13

COSTE, N.
25 Etudes, Op. 38 — Schott (GA)
Choose ANY ONE of
Nos. 1, 2, 10

GIULIANI, M.
24 Etudes, Op. 48 — Schott (GA)
Choose ANY ONE of
Nos. 5, 6, 12
Studi Per Chitarra — Zerboni
Choose ANY ONE of
Opus 30, No. 32
Opus 48, No. 14

SAGRERAS, J.
Las cuartas lecciones — Guitar Heritage
Choose ANY ONE of
Nos. 18, 20, 24, 25
Les quintas lecciones — Guitar Heritage
Choose ANY ONE of
Nos. 1, 4, 6

SOR, F./SEGOVIA
Twenty Studies: — Marks Music
Choose ANY ONE of
Nos. 6, 7

TANSMAN, A.
12 Pieces Faciles, I — Eschig
No. 12: Trioles

TÁRREGA, F.
Etuden — Universal
Choose ANY ONE of
Nos. 7, 8

Supplementary Piece

Candidates must be prepared to play ONE Supplementary Piece. This piece need not be from the Syllabus lists, and may be chosen entirely at the discretion of the teacher and student. It may represent a period or style of piece not already included in the examination program, but which holds special interest for the candidate. The choice must be within the following guidelines:

1) The equivalent level of difficulty of the piece may be at a higher grade level, providing it is within the technical and musical grasp of the candidate.

2) Pieces below the equivalent of Grade 5 level of difficulty are not acceptable.

3) The piece must be for solo guitar. Duets and trios are not acceptable.

4) Candidates with exceptional talent for improvisation may wish to improvise upon a theme of their choice. In this case, items 1 and 2 (above) will apply. Marks will be given for originality, musical inventiveness, and structural unity.

5) Candidates may choose to play a piece of music from standard real book form chosen either from any "Fake" Book or from *40 Compositions in Standard Real Form*. In this case, items 1 and 2 (above) will apply. Candidates must play both the melody and a suitable accompaniment. Marks will be given for a stylistic performance.

Special approval is not required for the Supplementary Piece. However, poor suitability of the choice may be reflected in the mark. Memorization is encouraged, though NOT required.

Technical Tests

Conservatory Canada's booklet *Guitar Technique Book* (1999) contains notational examples for all technical requirements.

All technical tests must be played from memory, evenly, with good tone, logical fingering. Metronome markings should be regarded as *minimum* speeds. The number of octaves are as given in *Guitar Technique Book* (1999).

KEYS REQUIRED IN GRADE SIX

	New Keys	Review Keys
Major	F#, Db	Ab
Minor	d#, bb	f

SCALES

To be played from memory, ascending AND descending, in the keys stated.

Scale fingerings: Right hand, fingered i-m, m-a, and i-a (to be specified by the examiner), using rest and free stroke. Use only movable, closed string left-hand fingering (except open 6th string).

	Keys	*M.M.* $\downarrow=$	*Articulation*
Major	F#, Ab, Db,	66	in sixteenth notes AND triplet eighth notes
Melodic minor	d#, f, bb	66	in sixteenth notes AND triplet eighth notes
Harmonic minor	d#, f, bb	66	in sixteenth notes AND triplet eighth notes
Repeated Note	F#, Db, d#, bb	72	in sixteenth notes
Slur	D	80	compound in triplet eighth notes
3rd & 6th	C	60	solid in eighth notes
Chromatic	beginning on C	66	in sixteenth notes AND triplet eighth notes
Whole Tone	beginning on C	96	in eighth notes
Blues	beginning on G	92	in eighth notes

Note: Do NOT repeat the upper tonic note.
Do NOT play either the tonic chord or a cadence at the end of the scale.

TRIADS

To be played ascending AND descending in the keys stated.

	Keys	*Position*	*M.M.* $\downarrow=$	*Note Values*
Solid Triads (Major & Minor)	F#, Db, d#, bb	Root & Inversions	76	in quarter notes

ARPEGGIOS

To be played ascending AND descending in the keys stated.

	Keys	*Position*	*M.M.* ♩=	*Note Values*
Major	F#, Db	Root position	76	in eighth notes
Minor	d#, bb	Root position	76	in eighth notes
Dominant 7th	in the KEY OF F#, Db	Root position	76	in eighth notes
Diminished 7th	in the KEY OF d#, bb	Root position	76 66	in eighth notes

HARMONIZATION

Candidates are required to harmonize a simple melody at sight, ending with a Perfect or Plagal cadence as appropriate. The examiner will play the melody. The candidate will supply chords as indicated by an x. Chords may be strummed or played in solid form (*i.e.* p i m a)

        Keys of   C, G Major

        Chords   I and V OR I and IV.

Example

Sight Reading

Candidates are required to perform at sight a) a rhythmic exercise and b) a passage of guitar score as described below. The candidate will be given a brief period to scan the score, but not to "practise silently" before beginning to play. Candidates must perform each section without counting aloud. It is recommended that candidates maintain a steady beat, and avoid the unnecessary repetition caused by attempting to correct errors during the performance.

a) Rhythm	*b) Guitar Passage*
To tap, clap or play on one note (at the candidate's choice) a simple rhythm.	To play at sight a short piece about equal in difficulty to pieces of Grade 3-4 level.
Length 4 bars Time signature 3/4, 4/4 Note values variety of values including triplets and ties Rest values whole, 1/2, 1/4, 1/8	Keys Major & Minor up to and including 3 sharps or flats. Length 8-16 bars

Example: a) Rhythm

Aural Tests

The candidate will be required:

i) at the candidate's choice, to play back OR sing back to any vowel, a short melody of six to eight notes, in 2/4, 3/4 or 4/4 time, based on the first five notes and the lower leading tone in a *major* or *minor* key, after the Examiner has:

    ✓ named the key [up to and including two sharps or flats]
    ✓ played the 4-note chord on the tonic in broken form
    ✓ played the melody twice.

The melody will begin on the tonic note. Following is the approximate level of difficulty:

ii) to identify any of the following intervals after the Examiner has played each one once in broken form:

ABOVE a note	**BELOW a note**
major and minor 2nd	*major and minor 3rd*
major and minor 3rd	*perfect 4th*
perfect 4th	*perfect 5th*
perfect 5th	*minor 6th*
major and minor 6th	*perfect octave*
perfect octave	

iii) to identify any of the following triads/chords when played once by the Examiner in solid form, in close, root position:

    major and *minor* triads (3-note)
    dominant 7th chords (4-note)
    diminished 7th chords (4-note)

iv) to state whether a short piece in *chorale* style is in a *major* or a *minor* key, and whether the final cadence is **Perfect** (V-I), **Plagal** (IV-I), or **Interrupted/Deceptive** (V-VI).

Viva Voce

Candidates must be prepared to give verbal answers to questions on the THREE List pieces selected for the examination. Candidates must ensure that all teaching notes and other written comments are removed from the score before the examination. The questions will include the following elements:

i) to find and explain all of the signs (including clefs, time signatures, key signatures, accidentals, etc.), articulation markings (legato, staccato, accents, phrase or slur markings, etc.), dynamic and tempo markings, and other musical terms as they may be found in the three selected pieces.

ii) without reference to the score, to give the title, key and composer of the piece.

iii) to explain the meaning of the title of the piece.

iv) to give a few relevant details about the composer (List A and List B only).

v) with direct reference to the score, to explain briefly the form of the piece (for example, binary or ternary form, dance piece, sonata, etc.)

vi) with direct reference to the score, to explain briefly the key structure, including any modulations.

Length of the examination:	30 minutes
Examination Fee:	Please consult the current examination application form for the schedule of fees.
Co-requisite:	Successful completion of the following written examination is required for the awarding of the Grade 7 Practical Certificate.

Theory 3

Requirements & Marking

Requirement	Total Marks
FOUR LIST PIECES	
To be performed from memory	
1 from List A	11
1 from List B	11
2 from List C (10 marks each)	20
ONE STUDY	9
ONE SUPPLEMENTARY PIECE	7
TECHNICAL TESTS	
Scales, Triads, Arpeggios	14
Harmonization	4
SIGHT READING	
Rhythm Pattern	2
Guitar Passage	6
AURAL TESTS	8
VIVA VOCE (List Pieces only)	4
MARKS FOR MEMORY	4
List pieces only (1 mark each)	
TOTAL POSSIBLE MARKS	100

Pieces

Candidates must be prepared to play FOUR pieces, one from *List A*, one from *List B*, and two from *List C*, chosen to contrast in style, key, tempo, etc.. Your choice must include FOUR different composers. All pieces must be performed from memory.

LIST A

ANONYMOUS
As I went to Walsingham — Ariel Music
(The Renaissance Guitar)
BACH, J.S.
Cello Suite No. 1, BWV 1007 — Any edition
Choose ANY ONE of
Minuets I AND II
Sarabande
Sarabande *(Lute Suite, BWV 995)* — Any edition
Praeludium für Lauten, BWV 999 — Any edition
DOWLAND, J.
Captain Digori Piper's Galliard — Any edition
HÄNDEL, G.F./SEGOVIA
Eight Aylesford Pieces — Schott (GA)
Choose ANY ONE of
Menuet I AND II
Gavotte
HOLBORNE, A.
Galliard *(The Renaissance Guitar)* — Ariel Music
The Nightwatch — Ariel Music
(The Renaissance Guitar)
MILAN, L.
Fantasia de Consonancias Y Redobles — Any edition
MUDARRA, A.
Differencias sobre - El Conde Claros — Any edition
Galliard *(The Renaissance Guitar)* — Ariel Music
NARVAEZ, L. DE
Cancion del Emperador sobra -Mille Regres — Any edition
PILKINGTON, F.
Mrs. Anne Harecourt's Galliard — Ariel Music
(The Renaissance Guitar)
PURCELL, H./BREAM
Rondo *(Four Pieces)* — Faber
ROSSETER, P.
Galliard *(The Renaissance Guitar)* — Ariel Music
SANZ, G.
Canarios — Colombo
SCARLATTI, D.
Sonata, K 391 — Waterloo
SCARLATTI, D./DUARTE
Sonata,, K291/L6 *(Four Sonatas)* — Universal
TELEMAN, G.P.
Allegro AND Presto *(Fantasia No. 5)* — Waterloo
WEISS, S.L.
Sonata in D minor (Dresden No. 5) — Universal
Choose ANY ONE of
Bourree
Gigue
Prelude & Toccata *(Partita No. 15)* — Schott
Eleven Pieces from the
London Manuscripts — Ricordi
Choose ANY ONE of
Nos. 7, 10

LIST B

ANONYMOUS
Three Catalonian Melodies — Universal
Choose ANY ONE
COSTE, N.
Berceuse *(Guitar Works, IX)* — Chanterelle

DIABELLI, A.
Three Sonatas — Schott
Choose ANY ONE of
Sonata in C
(EITHER 1st mov't OR 2nd mov't)
Sonata in A
(EITHER 2nd mov't OR 3rd mov't)
GIULIANI, M.
Le Bouquet emblèmatique — Ricordi
Choose ANY ONE of
Le myrte
La pensée
Le romarin
La violette
LAGOYA, A.
Reverie in D — Ricordi
MOZART, W.A./SEGOVIA
Menuet *(Guitar Archive No. 117)* — Schott (GA)
MERTZ, J.K.
Trois Nocturnes, Op. 4 — Chanterelle
Choose ANY ONE
PAGANINI, N.
Kleine Stucke — Zimmerman
Choose ANY ONE of
Nos. 9, 24
SCHUMANN, R./SEGOVIA
Romanza *(Album of Guitar Solos)* — Colombo
SOR, F.
Variations on a Scottish Theme, Op. 40 — Tecla
TÁRREGA, F.
Prelude 2 — Ricordi
Mazurka in Sol — Ricordi
Marietta — Ricordi
SATIE, E./PARKENING
Gymnopedie No. 1 — Brener
(Virtuoso Music for Guitar, II)

LIST C

ARNHEIM, TOBIAS & LEMARE
Sweet and Lovely *(Concepts)* — Big 3 Music
BARRIOS, A. MANGORE
Oracion por todos *(Guitar Works, I)* — Belwin
Preludio *(Guitar Works, I)* — Belwin
BENEDICT, R.
Divertimenti: No. 8 — Waterloo
BERGMAN & LEGARND
Sweet Gingerbread Man *(Concepts)* — Big 3 Music
BRINDLE, R. SMITH
El Polifemo de Oro: — Bruzzichelli
Choose ANY ONE of
Nos. 1, 3
BROUWER, L.
Berceuse — Eschig
(Deux Themes Populaires Cubains)
BRULE, P.M.
Rapsodie Pour Guitarre — Waterloo
CARLEVARO, A.
Campo *(Preludios Americanos)* — Barry Buenos
DARCH, C.
Opera House Rag *(Guitar Workshop)* — Presser
DE FALLA, M..
Récit de pêcheur *(Two Pièces)* — Chester

38

DUBY & BONFA
  The Gentle Rain *(Concepts)* — Big 3 Music
FIELDS & MCHUGH
  Don't Blame Me *(Concepts)* — Big 3 Music
HARRIS, A.
  Suite of Seven Pieces — Colombo
  Choose ANY TWO
LAURO, A.
  Quatro valses Venezolanos — Brock
  Choose ANY ONE of
    Nos. 1, 2
PARISH, MALNECK & SIGNORELLI
  Stairway to the Stars *(Concepts)* — Big 3 Music
MARTIN, F.
  Air *(Quatro Pièces brèves)* — Universal

ROGERS & HART
  Blue Moon *(Concepts)* — Big 3 Music
TOROK, A.
  Sketches from Life — Waterloo
  Choose ANY ONE of
    Modern Additives
    Ich Auch
VILLA-LOBOS
  Prélude I — Eschig
  Suite populaire brésilienne — Eschig
  Choose ANY ONE of
    Mazurka - Choro
    Valsa - Choro

Studies

Candidates must be prepared to play ONE study chosen from the following List. Memorization is recommended though NOT required.

STUDY LIST

AGUADO
  Studi per Chitarra — Zerboni
  Choose ANY ONE of
    Nos. 38, 39
BARRIOS, A. MANGORE
  Guitar Works, I — Belwin
  Choose ANY ONE of
    Estudio Inconcluso
    Estudio de Legado
    Estudio en arpeggio
CARCASSI, M.
  25 Melodious Studies, Op. 60 — Fisher
  Choose ANY ONE of
    Nos. 17, 19
COSTE, N.
  25 Etudes, Op. 38 — Schott (GA)
  Choose ANY ONE of
    Nos. 4, 7, 11, 12, 18

PRESTI, I.
  Six Etudes Pour Guitar — Eschig
  Choose ANY ONE of
    Nos. 1, 2, 3
SAGRERAS, J.
  Las Quntas Lecciones — Guitar Heritage
  Choose ANY ONE of
    Nos. 19, 26, 30, 40
SOR, F/SEGOVIA
  Twenty Studies — Marks Music
  Choose ANY ONE of
    Nos. 1 to 8
VILLA-LOBOS, H.
  Douze Etudes — Eschig
  Choose ANY ONE of
    Nos. 1, 7

Supplementary Piece

Candidates must be prepared to play ONE Supplementary Piece. This piece need not be from the Syllabus lists, and may be chosen entirely at the discretion of the teacher and student. It may represent a period or style of piece not already included in the examination program, but which holds special interest for the candidate. The choice must be within the following guidelines:

1) The equivalent level of difficulty of the piece may be at a higher grade level, providing it is within the technical and musical grasp of the candidate.

2) Pieces below the equivalent of Grade 6 level of difficulty are not acceptable.

3) The piece must be for solo guitar. Duets and trios are not acceptable.

4) Candidates with exceptional talent for improvisation may wish to improvise upon a theme of their choice. In this case, items 1 and 2 (above) will apply. Marks will be given for originality, musical inventiveness, and structural unity.

5) Candidates may choose to play a piece of music from standard real book form chosen either from any "Fake" Book or from *40 Compositions in Standard Real Form*. In this case, items 1 and 2 (above) will apply. Candidates must play both the melody and a suitable accompaniment. Marks will be given for a stylistic performance.

Special approval is not required for the Supplementary Piece. However, poor suitability of the choice may be reflected in the mark. Memorization is encouraged, though NOT required.

Technical Tests
Conservatory Canada's booklet *Guitar Technique Book* (1999) contains notational examples for all technical requirements.

All technical tests must be played from memory, evenly, with good tone, logical fingering. Metronome markings should be regarded as *minimum* speeds. The number of octaves are as given in *Guitar Technique Book* (1999).

KEYS REQUIRED IN GRADE SEVEN

	New Keys
Major	ALL keys
Minor	ALL keys

SCALES
To be played from memory, ascending AND descending, in the keys stated.

Scale fingerings: Right hand, fingered i-m, m-a, and i-a (to be specified by the examiner), using rest and free stroke. Use only movable, closed string left-hand fingering (except open 6th string).

	Keys	M.M. ♩=	Articulation
Major	All keys	80	in sixteenth notes AND triplet eighth notes
Melodic minor	All keys	80	in sixteenth notes AND triplet eighth notes
Harmonic minor	All keys	80	in sixteenth notes AND triplet eighth notes
Slur	G	104	compound in triplet eighth notes
Repeated	D, F#, Db d#, g#, bb	72	in quintuplet sixteenth notes
3rd & 6th	G	66	solid form in eighth notes
Chromatic	beginning on G	80	in sixteenth notes AND triplet eighth notes
Pentatonic	beginning on D	104	in eighth notes
Blues	beginning on G	104	in eighth notes

Note: Do NOT repeat the upper tonic note.

                     Do NOT play either the tonic chord or a cadence at the end of the scale.

TRIADS

To be played ascending AND descending in the keys stated.

	Keys	*Position*	*M.M.* $\downarrow$ =	*Note Values*
Solid Triads (Major & Minor)	C, G, F a, e, d	Root & inversions	80	in quarter notes

ARPEGGIOS

To be played ascending AND descending in the keys stated.

	Keys	*Position*	*M.M.* $\downarrow$ =	*Note Values*
Major	C, G, D, F, B$\flat$		80	in eighth notes
Minor	a, e, b, d, g		80	in eighth notes
Dominant 7th	in the KEY OF C, G, D, F, Bb		80	in eighth notes
Diminished 7th	in the KEY OF a, e, b, d, g		80	in eighth notes

HARMONIZATION

Candidates are required to harmonize a simple melody at sight, ending with a Perfect or Plagal cadence as appropriate. The examiner will play the melody. The candidate will supply chords as indicated by an x. Chords may be strummed or played in solid form (*i.e.* p i m a)

Keys of   C, G Major

                    a minor

Chords   I, IV, V

                    i, iv, V

Sight Reading

Candidates are required to perform at sight a) a rhythmic exercise and b) a passage of guitar score as described below. The candidate will be given a brief period to scan the score, but not to "practise silently" before beginning to play. Candidates must perform each section without counting aloud. It is recommended that candidates maintain a steady beat, and avoid the unnecessary repetition caused by attempting to correct errors during the performance.

a) **Rhythm**	b) **Guitar Passage**
To tap, clap or play on one note (at the candidate's choice) a simple rhythm. Length 4 bars Time signature 2/4, 3/4, 6/8 Note values variety of values including ties Rest values variety of values	To play at sight a short guitar piece about equal in difficulty to pieces of Grade 4-5 level. Keys Major & Minor up to and including 3 sharps or flats. Length 8-16 bars

Example: a) Rhythm

Aural Tests

The candidate will be required:

i) at the candidate's choice, to play back OR sing back to any vowel, a short melody of six to eight notes, in 2/4, 3/4, 4/4, or 6/8 time, based on the first six notes and the lower leading tone in a *major* or *minor* key, after the Examiner has:
✓named the key [up to and including three sharps or flats]
✓played the 4-note chord on the tonic in broken form
✓played the melody twice.

The melody will begin on the tonic note. Only the harmonic form of the minor will be used. Following is the approximate level of difficulty:

ii) to identify any of the following intervals after the Examiner has played each one once in broken form:

ABOVE a note
major and minor 2nd
major and minor 3rd
perfect 4th
perfect 5th
major and minor 6th
minor 7th
perfect octave

BELOW a note
major and minor 3rd
perfect 4th
perfect 5th
major and minor 6th
perfect octave

iii) to identify any of the following triads/chords when played once by the Examiner in solid form, in close, root position:
major and *minor* triads (3-note)
augmented triads (3-note)
dominant 7th chords (4-note)
diminished 7th chords (4-note)

iv) to state whether a short piece in *chorale* style is in a *major* or a *minor* key, and whether the final cadence is **Perfect** (V-I), **Imperfect** (I-V only), **Plagal** (IV-I), or **Interrupted/Deceptive** (V-VI).

Viva Voce

Candidates must be prepared to give verbal answers to questions on the FOUR List pieces selected for the examination. Candidates must ensure that all teaching notes and other written comments are removed from the score before the examination. The questions will include the following elements:

i) to find and explain all of the signs (including clefs, time signatures, key signatures, accidentals, etc.), articulation markings (legato, staccato, accents, phrase or slur markings, etc.), dynamic and tempo markings, and other musical terms as they may be found in the three selected pieces.

ii) without reference to the score, to give the title, key and composer of the piece.

iii) to explain the meaning of the title of the piece.

iv) to give a few relevant details about the composer (List A, and List B only).

v) with direct reference to the score, to explain briefly the form of the piece (for example, binary or ternary form, dance piece, sonata, etc.)

vi) with direct reference to the score, to explain briefly the key structure, including any modulations.

GRADE EIGHT

Length of the examination: 40 minutes

Examination Fee: Please consult the current examination application form for the schedule of fees.

Co-requisite: Successful completion of the following written examination is required for the awarding of the Grade 8 Practical Certificate.
Theory 4

Requirements & Marking

Requirement	Total Marks
FOUR LIST PIECES	
To be performed from memory	
1 from List A	11
1 from List B	11
2 from List C (10 marks each)	20
ONE STUDY	9
ONE SUPPLEMENTARY PIECE	7
TECHNICAL TESTS	
Scales, Triads, Arpeggios	14
Harmonization	4
SIGHT READING	
Rhythm Pattern	2
Guitar Passage	6
AURAL TESTS	8
VIVA VOCE (List Pieces only)	4
MEMORY (List Pieces only)	4
TOTAL POSSIBLE MARKS	100

Pieces

Candidates must be prepared to play FOUR pieces, one from *List A,* one from *List B,* and two from *List C,* chosen to contrast in style, key, tempo, etc.. Your choice must include FOUR different composers. All pieces must be performed from memory.

LIST A

ANONYMOUS
Go from my Window | Ariel Music
(The Renaissance Guitar)
BACH, J.S.
Andante | Any edition
(Violin Sonata, BWV 1003)
Prelude | Any edition
(Cello Suite No. 1, BWV 1007)
Lute Suite No. 1, BWV 996 | Any edition
Choose ANY ONE of
Courante
Allemande
Gavotte | Any edition
(Lute Suite No. 1, BWV 1006)
BALLARD, R.
Ballet de la Reyne | Biberian
(Guitar Solos from France)
CUTTING, F.
Almain *(The Renaissance Guitar)* | Ariel Music
Greensleeves | Ariel Music
(The Renaissance Guitar)
DE FUENLLANA, M.
Fantasia *(The Renaissance Guitar)* | Ariel Music
DE VISÉE, R.
Le Tombeau de Francois Corbetta | Eschig
DOWLAND, J.
The Renaissance Guitar | Ariel Music
Choose ANY ONE of
Melancholy Gilliard
Queen Elizabeth's Galliard
Lady Hammond's Alman
MUDARRA, A.
Fantasia X | Any edition
NARVAEZ, L. DE
Diferencias: sobra | Any edition
"Guardame las Vacas"
SCARLATTI, D.
Four Sonatas | Universal
Choose ANY ONE of
Sonata, K.301
Sonata, K.452
WEISS, S.L.
Minuet *(Six Lute Pieces, I)* | Colombo
Sonata in D minor (Dresden No. 5) | Universal
Choose ANY ONE of
Allemande
Courante

LIST B

AGUADO, D.
Aguado/Brevier | Schott
Choose ANY ONE of
Minuet I
Minuet II
Andante I
DIABELLI, A.
Three Sonatas | Schott
Sonata in A
(EITHER 1st mov't OR 4th mov't)
Sonata in F
(EITHER 1st mov't OR 3rd mov't)

GIULIANI, M.
Le bouquet emblèmatique | Ricordi
Choose ANY ONE of
Le lis
Le jasmin
L'oeillet
Le Narcisse
GRIEG, E./SEGOVIA
Melody, Op. 38, No. 3 | Colombo
(Album of Guitar Solos)
HAYDN, F.J.
Minuet *(Quartet in G, Hob: III/75)* | Schott
MERTZ, J.K.
Auf Enthalt *(Guitar Works, VII)* | Chanterelle
PAGANINI, N.
Romance | Universal
(Grand Sonata, in A, M.S. No. 3)
SCHUMANN, R./BREAM
Kindersonaten, Op. 118 | Faber
Choose ANY ONE of
Nos. 1, 2, 3
SOR, F.
Andante Largo, Op. 5, No. 5 | Universal
Folies d'Espagne, Op. 15, No. I | Ricordi
Fantasia, Op. 4, No. 2 | Oxford
TÁRREGA
Maria "Gavota" | Ricordi

LIST C

BARRIOS MANGORE, A.
Julia Florida | Belwin
BARNES, M.
Fantasy | Waterloo
Choose ANY ONE of
Meno Mosso
Molto Tenuto
Moderato
BENNETT, R.R.
Impromptu No. 3 *(Impromptus)* | Universal
BERGMAN & LEGRAND
What are you doing the rest
of your life *(Concepts)* | Big 3 Music
BREAU, L.
Freight Train | Mel Bay
BRINDLE, R. SMITH
No. 2 *(El Polifemo De Oro)* | Bruzzichelli
DODGSON, S.
Adagio *(Partita I for Guitar)* | Oxford
GRANADOS, E.
Villanesca No. 4 | Belwin Mills
(Four Spanish Dances Op. 37)
HAND, F.
Elegy for a King | Ricordi
LAURO, A.
Valse No. 3 | Broek
(Quatro Valses Venezolanos)
LLOBET, M.
Ten Catalan Folk Songs | Universal
Choose ANY ONE of
El Noy de la mare
Canco del Iladre
El Testament d'Amelia

MARTIN, F.
Prélude *(Quatre Pièces brèves)* — Universal
MARTIN & BLAIN.
Have yourself a Merry Little Christmas
(Concepts) — Big 3 Music
MOMPOU, F.
Suite Compostelana — Sol
Choose ANY ONE of
Cuna
Cancion
PASS, J.
Virtuoso III — Mel Bay
Choose ANY ONE of
Trinidad
Sultry
Dissonance No. 1
PIAZZOLLA, A.
Tanguisimo — Ed Margaux
Bueno Aires Hova Cero — Ed Margaux

PONCE, M.
Préludes, II — Tecla
Choose ANY TWO
RAZAF, GOODMAN, WEBB & SAMPSON
Stompin' at the Savoy *(Concepts)* — Big 3 Music
SEALY, R.
New York — Waterloo
SOMERS, H.
Finale *(Sonata for Guitar)* — Caveat
TANSMAN, A.
Sarabande (Cavatina) — Schott
Danza Pomposa — Schott
Choose ANY ONE of
Cavatina
Sarabande
TORROBA, F. MORENO
Fandanguillo *(Suite Castellana)* — Schott
VILLA-LOBOS, H.
Prélude 3 — Eschig
Prélude 5 — Eschig
Choro-Typico — Columbia

Studies

Candidates must be prepared to play ONE Study chosen from the following List. Memorization is recommended though NOT required.

STUDY LIST

AGUADO, D.
Studi per Chitarra — Zerboni
Choose ANY ONE of
Nos. 41, 42
CARCASSI, M.
25 Melodious Studies, Op. 60 — C. Fisher
Choose ANY ONE of
Nos. 20, 22, 23
COSTE, N.
25 Etudes, Op. 38 — Schott
Choose ANY ONE of
Nos. 3, 5, 6, 17, 19, 23

PRESTI, I.
Six Etudes Pour Guitar — Eschig
Choose ANY ONE of
Nos. 4, 5, 6
SOR, F./SEGOVIA
Twenty Studies — Marks Music
Choose ANY ONE of
No. 10, 11, 15
VILLA-LOBOS
Etude No. 8 *(Douze Etudes)* — Eschig

Supplementary Piece

Candidates must be prepared to play ONE Supplementary Piece. This piece need not be from the Syllabus lists, and may be chosen entirely at the discretion of the teacher and student. It may represent a period or style of piece not already included in the examination program, but which holds special interest for the candidate. The choice must be within the following guidelines:

1) The equivalent level of difficulty of the piece may be at a higher grade level, providing it is within the technical and musical grasp of the candidate.

2) Pieces below the equivalent of Grade 7 level of difficulty are not acceptable.

3) The piece must be for solo guitar. Duets and trios are not acceptable.

4) Candidates with exceptional talent for improvisation may wish to improvise upon a theme of their choice. In this case, items 1 and 2 (above) will apply. Marks will be given for originality, musical inventiveness, and structural unity.

5) Candidates may choose to play a piece of music from standard real book form chosen either from any "Fake" Book or from *40 Compositions in Standard Real Form*. In this case, items 1 and 2 (above) will apply. Candidates must play both the melody and a suitable accompaniment. Marks will be given for a stylistic performance.

Special approval is not required for the Supplementary Piece. However, poor suitability of the choice may be reflected in the mark. Memorization is encouraged, though NOT required.

Technical Tests

Conservatory Canada's booklet *Guitar Technique Book* (1999) contains notational examples for all technical requirements.

All technical tests must be played from memory, evenly, with good tone, logical fingering. Metronome markings should be regarded as *minimum* speeds. The number of octaves are as given in *Guitar Technique Book* (1999).

KEYS REQUIRED IN GRADE EIGHT

	New Keys
Major	All Keys
Minor	All Keys

SCALES

To be played from memory, ascending AND descending, in the keys stated.

Scale fingerings: Right hand, fingered i-m, m-a, and i-a (to be specified by the examiner), using rest and free stroke. Use only movable, closed string left-hand fingering (except open 6th string).

	Keys	*M.M.* $\downarrow$ =	*Articulation*
Major	All keys	92	triplet eighth notes AND triplet sixteenth notes
Melodic minor	All keys	92	triplet eighth notes AND triplet sixteenth notes
Harmonic minor	All keys	92	triplet eighth notes AND triplet sixteenth notes
Repeated	All keys	69	sextuplet sixteenth notes
Slur	C, A	116	compound, triplet eight notes
3rd & 6th	D	80	solid in eighth notes AND broken in sixteenth notes
Chromatic	beginning on E♭	92	triplet eighth notes AND triplet sixteenth notes
Pentatonic	beginning on D	120	in eighth notes
Whole Tone/Half Tone	beginning on A	112	in eighth notes

Note: Do NOT repeat the upper tonic note.
Do NOT play either the tonic chord or a cadence at the end of the scale.

TRIADS

To be played ascending AND descending in the keys stated.

	Keys	*Position*	*M.M.* ♩=	*Note Values*
Solid Triads (Major & Minor)	D, A, B♭ b, f#, g#	Root & Inversions	84	in quarter notes

ARPEGGIOS

To be played ascending AND descending in the keys stated.

	Keys	*Position*	*M.M.* ♩=	*Note Values*
Major	A, E, B, Eb, Ab		92	in eighth notes
Minor	f#, c#, g#, c, f		92	in eighth notes
Dominant 7th	in the KEY OF A, E, B, Eb, Ab		92	in eighth notes in triplet eighth notes
Diminished 7th	in the KEY OF f#, c#, g#, c, f		92	in eighth notes

HARMONIZATION

Candidates are required to harmonize a simple melody at sight, ending with a Perfect or Plagal cadence as appropriate. The examiner will play the melody and the candidate is expected to provide a suitable continuous accompaniment similar to (but not limited to) the following styles:

Example

Chords will be indicated by an x..

Keys of   G, D, A Major
            e minor
Chords   I, i, IV, iv, V or V⁷

Sight Reading

Candidates are required to perform at sight a) a rhythmic exercise and b) a passage of guitar score as described below. The candidate will be given a brief period to scan the score, but not to "practise silently" before beginning to play. Candidates must perform each section without counting aloud. It is recommended that candidates maintain a steady beat, and avoid the unnecessary repetition caused by attempting to correct errors during the performance.

a) Rhythm	b) Guitar Passage
To tap or play on one note (at the candidate's choice) a rhythm in simple or compound time. May include syncopated rhythms. Length 4-8 bars Time signature any simple OR compound time Note values variety of values including triplets and ties Rest values variety of values	To play at sight a short guitar piece equal in difficulty to pieces of Grade 5-6 level, in any style or period. Keys Major & Minor up to and including 4 sharps or flats. Length 8-16 bars

Example: a) Rhythm

Aural Tests

The candidate will be required:

i) at the candidate's choice, to play back OR sing back to any vowel, a short melody of eight to twelve notes, in 2/4, 3/4, 4/4, or 6/8 time, in a *major* or *minor* key, within the range of one octave after the Examiner has:
    ✓ named the key [up to and including three sharps or flats]
    ✓ played the 4-note chord on the tonic in broken form
    ✓ played the melody twice.

The melody may begin on ANY note of the tonic chord. Only the harmonic form of the minor will be used. Following is the approximate level of difficulty:

ii) to identify any of the following intervals after the Examiner has played each one once in broken form:

ABOVE a note
major and minor 2nd
major and minor 3rd
perfect 4th
perfect 5th
major and minor 6th
major and minor 7th
perfect octave

BELOW a note
major and minor 2nd
major and minor 3rd
perfect 4th
perfect 5th
major and minor 6th
major and minor
perfect octave

iii)   to identify any of the following triads/chords when played once by the Examiner in solid
form, in close, root position:

> *major* and *minor* triads (3-note)
> *augmented* triads (3-note)
> *diminished* triads (3-note)
> *dominant 7th* chords (4-note)
> *diminished 7th* chords (4-note)

iv)   to state whether a short piece in *chorale* style is in a *major* or a *minor* key, and whether   both the
final cadence AND one internal cadence are **Perfect** (V-I), **Imperfect** (I-V, II-V, and IV-V),
Plagal (IV-I), or **Interrupted/Deceptive** (V-VI).   The Examiner will play the passage TWICE;
the first time straight through without interruption, the second time stopping at the internal
cadence point for the candidate to identify it.

Viva Voce

Candidates must be prepared to give verbal answers to questions on the FOUR List pieces selected for
the examination.   Candidates must ensure that all teaching notes and other written comments are
removed from the score before the examination. The questions will include the following elements:

i)   to find and explain all of the signs (including clefs, time signatures, key signatures,
accidentals, etc.), articulation markings (legato, staccato, accents, phrase or slur markings, etc.),
dynamic and tempo markings, and other musical terms as they may be found in the three selected
pieces.

ii)   without reference to the score, to give the title, key and composer of the piece.

iii)   to explain the meaning of the title of the piece.

iv)   to give a few relevant details about the composer (List A, and List B only).

v)   with direct reference to the score, to explain briefly the form of the piece (for example, binary or
ternary form, dance piece, sonata, etc.)

vi)   with direct reference to the score, to explain briefly the key structure, including any
modulations.

vii)   to answer general questions about the history and construction of the guitar and its
predecessors.

*NOTE: Candidates taking a Partial Examination MUST include Viva Voce in the same part with
the last List Piece, and*
> *i)   be prepared to answer questions on ALL FOUR List Pieces;*
> *ii)   provide music for ALL FOUR List Pieces.*

Length of the examination:	40 minutes
Examination Fee:	Please consult the current examination application form for the schedule of fees.
Co-requisite:	Successful completion of the following written examinations is required for the awarding of the Grade 9 Practical Certificate.

Theory 5 AND *History 5 or History 6*

Requirements & Marking

Requirement	Total Marks
FIVE LIST PIECES	
To be performed from memory	
1 from List A	10
1 from List B	10
2 from List C (10 marks each)	20
1 from either List A or List B	10
ONE STUDY	9
ONE SUPPLEMENTARY PIECE	7
TECHNICAL TESTS	
Scales, Arpeggios	14
Harmonization	4
SIGHT READING	
Rhythm Pattern	2
Guitar Passage	6
AURAL TESTS	8
MEMORY (included in marks for List Pieces)	--
TOTAL POSSIBLE MARKS	100

Pieces

Candidates must be prepared to play FIVE pieces, one from *List A,* one from *List B*, and two from *List C*, and one additional piece from either *List A* or *List B*, chosen to contrast in style, key, tempo, etc.. Your choice must include FIVE different composers. All pieces must be performed from memory.

LIST A

BACH, J.S.
Prelude — Any edition
(Prelude, Fugue, and Allegro, BWV 998)
Gigue *(Lute Suite, BWV 996)* — Any edition
Allemande *(Lute Suite, BWV 995)* — Any edition

BATCHELAR, D.
Almaine *(International Anthology)* — Colombo

CIMAROSA, D./BREAM
Sonata No. 2 *(Three Sonatas)* — Faber

HOLBORNE, A.
Prelude and Fantasia — NovaScribe

SCARLATTI, D.
Sonata, L.395 — Colombo

WEISS, S.L.
Six Lute Pieces, II (Lima) — Colombo
  Choose ANY ONE of
    Chaconne
    Sarabande
    Prelude
Fantasie — Universal
Tombeau sur la Morte de M. Comte de Logy — Universal
Passacaglia — Universal

LIST B

AGUADO, D
Aguado/Brevier — Schott
  Choose ANY ONE OF
    Andante II
    Andante III
    Minuet III

GIULIANI, M.
Follia di Spagna, Op. 45 — Zerboni
(Variazioni sur Tema della)
"La risoluzione" *(Giulianate No. 1, Op. 148)* — Zerboni

MANJON, A.J.
Cuento de Amor — Chanterelle

SOR, F.
Fantasie, Op. 10 — Tecla
Grand Solo, Op. 14 — Zerboni
Grand Sonate, Op. 22 — Zerboni
  (EITHER 2nd mov't OR 4th mov't)
Sonata, Op. 15 No. 2 (complete) — Zerboni

LIST C

ALBENIZ, I.
Asturias, Op. 4, No. 1 — Columbia
Granada *(Suite Espanola, Op. 181, No. I)* — Belwin

ARCHER, V.
Fantasie on "Blanche comme la Neige" — Columbia

BARIOS MANGORE, A.
Allegro *(La Cathédrale)* — Belwin

BENNETT, R.R.
Impromptu No. 11 — Universal

BREAU, L.
Five O'Clock Bells — Mel Bay

BRINDLE, R. SMITH
No. 4 *(El Polifemo De Oro)* — Bruzzichelli
November Memories — Zerboni

BROUWER, L.
Danza Caracteristica — Schott
Elogia de la Danza — Schott

DEBUSSY, C./PARKENING
The Girl with the Flaxen Hair — Sherry-Brenner
(Virtuoso Music for Guitar)

DE FALLA, M.
Homenaje — Ricordi

GRANADOS, E.
Danza España — Ricordi
  Choose ANY ONE of
    Nos. 3, 5

KRENCK, E.
Suite — Doblinger
  Choose ANY TWO Movements

MAXWELL-DAVIES, P.
Lullaby for Ilian Rainbow — Boosey & Hawkes

MOMPOU, F.
Suite Compostellana — Salabert
  Choose ANY ONE of
    Muñeira
    Préludio

PASS, J.
Virtuoso III — Mel Bay
  Choose ANY ONE of
    Dissonance No 2
    Minor Detail

PONCE, M.
Prélude in E, "in the style of Weiss" — Berben

RODRIGO, J.
En los trigales — Editions musicales
Sarabande Lointaine a la
  vihuela de Luis Milan (Pujol) — Eschig
Zapateado No. 3 *(Trés Pièces Españolas)* — Schott

TANSMAN, A.
Préludio *AND* Scherzino *(Cavatina)* — Schott

TÁRREGA, F.
Capricco Arabe — Any edition
Recuerdos de la Alhambra — Any edition

TORROBA, F. MORENO
Pièces caractéristiques — Schott
  Choose ANY ONE of
    Los Mayos
    Albada
    Panorama

TURINA, J.
Fandanguillo — Schott
Ráfaga — Schott

VILLA-LOBOS, H.
Prelude No. 2 — Eschig

WALTON, W.
Five Bagatelles — Oxford
  Choose ANY ONE of
    Nos. 3, 4

GRADE 9

Studies

Candidates must be prepared to play ONE Study chosen from the following List. Memorization is recommended though NOT required.

STUDY LIST

AGUADO, D
Studi per Chitarra — Zerboni
No. 49

BARRIOS MANGORE, A.
Guitar Works, II — Belwin
Estudio No. 3

CARCASSI, M.
Twenty Five Melodious and Progressive Studies, Op. 60 — Fisher
Choose ANY ONE of
Nos. 24, 25

COSTE, N.
25 Etudes — Schott
Choose ANY ONE of
Nos. 9, 16, 20, 21

DODGSON & QUINE
Studies, I — Ricordi
No. 4
Studies, II — Ricordi
Choose ANY ONE of
Nos. 14, 15

SOR, F/SEGOVIA
Twenty Studies — Marks Music
Choose ANY ONE of
Nos. 9, 14, 16

VILLA-LOBOS, H.
Douze Etudes — Eschig
Choose ANY ONE of
Nos. 4, 11, 12

Supplementary Piece

Candidates must be prepared to play ONE Supplementary Piece. This piece need not be from the Syllabus lists, and may be chosen entirely at the discretion of the teacher and student. It may represent a period or style of piece not already included in the examination program, but which holds special interest for the candidate. The choice must be within the following guidelines:

1) The equivalent level of difficulty of the piece may be at a higher grade level, providing it is within the technical and musical grasp of the candidate.

2) Pieces below the equivalent of Grade 8 level of difficulty are not acceptable.

3) The piece must be for solo guitar. Duets and trios are not acceptable.

4) Candidates with exceptional talent for improvisation may wish to improvise upon a theme of their choice. In this case, items 1 and 2 (above) will apply. Marks will be given for originality, musical inventiveness, and structural unity.

5) Candidates may choose to play a piece of music from standard real book form chosen either from any "Fake" Book or from *40 Compositions in Standard Real Form*. In this case, items 1 and 2 (above) will apply. Candidates must play both the melody and a suitable accompaniment. Marks will be given for a stylistic performance.

Special approval is not required for the Supplementary Piece. However, poor suitability of the choice may be reflected in the mark. Memorization is encouraged, though NOT required.

53

Technical Tests

Conservatory Canada's booklet *Guitar Technique Book* (1999) contains notational examples for all technical requirements.

All technical tests must be played from memory, evenly, with good tone, logical fingering. Metronome markings should be regarded as *minimum* speeds. The number of octaves are as given in *Guitar Technique Book* (1999).

KEYS REQUIRED IN GRADE NINE

	Keys
Major	ALL Keys
Minor	ALL Keys

SCALES

To be played from memory, ascending AND descending, in the keys stated.

Scale fingerings: Right hand, fingered i-m, m-a, and i-a (to be specified by the examiner), using rest and free stroke. Use only movable, closed string left-hand fingering (except open 6th string).

	Keys	M.M. ♩=	Articulation
Major	All keys	104 104	in sixteenth notes AND in triplet eighth notes
Minor (Harmonic AND Melodic)	All keys	104 104	in sixteenth notes AND in triplet eighth notes
Repeated	All keys	76	in quintuplet sixteenth notes AND in sextuplet sixteenth notes
Slur	G, A	132	in compound triplet eighth notes
3rd & 6th	A	88	solid in eighth notes AND broken in sixteenth notes
Chromatic	beginning on E	104	in sixteenth notes AND in triplet eighth notes

Note: Do NOT repeat the upper tonic note.
Do NOT play either the tonic chord or a cadence at the end of the scale.

TRIADS

None required.

ARPEGGIOS
To be played ascending AND descending in the keys stated.

	Keys	Position	M.M. ♩=	Note Values
Major	All keys		96	in eighth notes
Minor	All keys		96	in eighth notes
Dominant 7th	All keys (Major and Minor)		96	in eighth notes
Diminished 7th	All Minor keys		96	in eighth notes

HARMONIZATION
Candidates are required to harmonize a simple melody at sight, ending with a Perfect or Plagal cadence as appropriate. The examiner will play the melody and the candidate is expected to provide a suitable continuous accompaniment similar to (but not limited to) the following styles:

No indication of chord changes will be given.

Keys of   D, A, E Major
                  b minor

Chords   I, i, IV, iv, V or V^7

Sight Reading
Candidates are required to perform at sight a) a rhythmic exercise and b) a passage of guitar score as described below. The candidate will be given a brief period to scan the score, but not to "practise silently" before beginning to play. Candidates must perform each section without counting aloud. It is recommended that candidates maintain a steady beat, and avoid the unnecessary repetition caused by attempting to correct errors during the performance.

a) Rhythm	b) Guitar Passage
To tap, clap or play on one note (at the candidate's choice) a rhythm in simple or compound time. May include syncopated rhythms, changing-meters, and complex patterns, but not irregular meters. Length — 4 bars Time signature — any simple OR compound time Note values — variety of values including ties Rest values — variety of values	To play at sight a short guitar piece equal in difficulty to pieces of Grade 6-7 level, in any style or period. May include changing meters, but not irregular meters Keys — Major & Minor to 5 sharps and flats Length — 16-24 bars

Example: a) Rhythm

Aural Tests

The candidate will be required:

i) at the candidate's choice, to play back OR sing back to any vowel, the **upper** part of a two-part phrase in a major key, after the Examiner has:
    ✓ named the key [up to and including three sharps or flats]
    ✓ played the 4-note chord on the tonic in solid form
    ✓ played the passage twice.

The parts may begin on ANY note of the tonic chord. Following is the approximate level of difficulty:

ii) to identify any of the following intervals after the Examiner has played each one once in broken form:

ABOVE a note	BELOW a note
major and minor 2nd	*major and minor 2nd*
major and minor 3rd	*major and minor 3rd*
perfect 4th	*perfect 4th*
augmented 4th (diminished 5th)	*augmented 4th (diminished 5th)*
perfect 5th	*perfect 5th*
major and minor 6th	*major and minor 6th*
major and minor 7th	*major and minor 7th*
perfect octave	*perfect octave*

iii) to identify any of the following 4-note chords, and name the position, after each has been played once by the Examiner.

major and *minor* chords: root position and first inversion [to be played in solid form, close position]
dominant 7th chords: root position only [to be played in solid form, open (SATB) position]
diminished 7th chords: root position only [to be played in solid form, open (SATB) position]

iv) to state whether a short piece in *chorale* style is in a *major* or a *minor* key, and whether the final cadence and any internal cadences are **Perfect** (V-I), **Imperfect** (I-V, II-V, IV-V), **Plagal** (IV-I), or **Interrupted/Deceptive** (V-VI). The Examiner will play the passage TWICE; the first time straight through without interruption, the second time stopping at cadence points for the candidate to identify them.

GRADE TEN

Length of the examination: 55 minutes

Examination Fee: Please consult the current examination application form
                               for the schedule of fees.

Co-requisite: Successful completion of the following written examination is
                               required for the awarding of the Grade 10 Practical Certificate.
                               Theory 6 AND ***History 5*** AND ***History 6***

*Note   Completion of Grade 10 is NOT required to proceed to the Associate Diploma. However, candidates who
        successfully complete Grade 10 will be exempt from the Associate Diploma technique providing they
        obtain a minimum total of 70% in each of Technical Tests, Sight Reading and Aural Tests.*

Requirements & Marking

Requirement	Total Marks
FIVE LIST PIECES	
To be performed from memory	
1 from List A	10
1 from List B	10
2 from List C (10 marks each)	20
1 from either List A or List B	10
ONE STUDY	9
ONE SUPPLEMENTARY PIECE	7
TECHNICAL TESTS	
Scales, Arpeggios	14
Harmonization	4
SIGHT READING	
Rhythm Pattern	2
Guitar Passage	6
AURAL TESTS	8
MEMORY (included in marks for List Pieces)	--
TOTAL POSSIBLE MARKS	100

*NOTE: **The examination program must include at least ONE work by a Canadian composer. The
        Canadian work may be chosen from the List Pieces (indicated by an asterisk) OR as the
        Supplementary Piece.***

Pieces

Candidates must be prepared to play FIVE pieces, one from *List A,* one from *List B*, and two from *List C*,
and one additional piece from either *List A* or *List B*, chosen to contrast in style, key, tempo, etc.. Your
choice must include FIVE different composers. All pieces must be performed from memory.

LIST A

BACH, J.S.
Fugue for Lute, BWV 1000 — Any edition
Lute Suites — Any edition
  Choose ANY TWO movements from ANY Suite
  not listed in previous grades
Cello Suites — Any edition
  Choose ANY TWO movements from ANY Suite
  not listed in previous grades
DOWLAND, J.
Fantasie *(International Anthology)* — Colombo
MILANO, F. DA/CHIESA
Fantasia *(Antologia di musica antico, I)* — Zerboni

LIST B

AGUADO, D.
Rondo 2 in A minor: Andante & Rondo — Chanterelle
(Trois Rondo Brillantes Op. 2)
ALBENIZ, I.
Cordoba (Lima) — Colombo
Mallorca (Segovia) — Colombo
Sevilla *(Suite España, Op. 165, No. 3)* — Schott
Zambra granadina (Segovia) — Colombo
CASTELNUOVO-TEDESCO
Capriccio Diabolico — Ricordi
Rondo — Schott
Suite, Op. 133 — Schott
  Choose ANY ONE of
    Preludio
    Capriccio
Tarantella — Ricordi
GIULIANI, M.
Variation su un Tema di Handel, Op. 107 — Zerboni
GRANADOS, E
La Maja de Goya — Ricordi
Danza española — Any edition
  Choose ANY ONE of
    Nos. 10, 12
PONCE, M.
Sonata Romantic — Schott
  (Choose EITHER 1st mov't OR 4th mov't)
Sonata Classic — Schott
  (Choose EITHER 1st mov't OR 4th mov't)
MANJON, A.J.
Aire Vasco — Chanterelle
RODRIGO, J.
Trés pièces Españolas — Schott
  Choose ANY ONE of
    Fandango
    Passacaglia

TORROBA, F. MORENO
Sonatina in A (1st mov't) — Ricordi
Arada and Danza *(Suite Castellana)* — Schott
TURINA, J.
Hommage à Tarrega — Schott

LIST C

BENNETT, R.R.
Impromptus — Universal
  Choose ANY ONE of
    Nos. 1, 2, 4
BERKELEY, M.
Sonatina, Op. 51 — Chester
  Choose ANY TWO movements
BREAU, L.
Little Blues — Mel Bay
BROUWER, L.
Canticum — Schott
La espiral eterna — Schott
DODGSON, S.
Etude Caprice — Doberman
Fantasy - Divisions — Doberman
DOMENICONI, C.
Variations on a Turkish Theme — Bote & Bock
EASTWOOD, T.
Ballade: Fantasy No. 1 — Faber
HARRIS, A.
Sonatina — Colombia
  (Choose EITHER 1st mov't OR 3rd mov't)
HENZE, H.W.
Drei Tentos — Schott
  Choose ANY ONE
*MOREL, F.
Mi duele España — CMC
Tropes pour quito — CMC
  Choose ANY FOUR movements
PASS, J.
Virtuoso III — Mel Bay
  Choose ANY ONE of
    9ths
    Offbeat
    7ths
    Passanova
    Nina's Blues
    Pasta Blues
*SOMERS, H.
Prelude and Scherzo *(Sonata for Guitar)* — Caveat
TAKEMITSU, T.
All in Twilight — Schott
  Play Nos.1 AND 3

Studies

Candidates must be prepared to play ONE Study chosen from the following List. Memorization is recommended though NOT required.

STUDY LIST

AGUADO, D.
Studi per Chitarra   Zerboni
Choose ANY ONE of
Nos. 50, 51
COSTE, N.
25 Etudes, Op. 38   Schott
Choose ANY ONE of
Nos. 14, 15, 24
DODGSON & QUINE
Studies for Guitar, I   Ricordi
No. 10
Studies for Guitar, II   Ricordi
Choose ANY ONE of
Nos. 11, 13

MANJON, A.J.
Study in B flat minor   Chanterelle
SOR, F./SEGOVIA
Twenty Studies   Marks Music
Choose ANY ONE of
Nos. 12, 18, 20
VILLA-LOBOS, H.
Douze Etudes   Eschig
Choose ANY ONE of
Nos. 2, 3, 9, 10

Supplementary Piece

Candidates must be prepared to play ONE Supplementary Piece. This piece need not be from the Syllabus lists, and may be chosen entirely at the discretion of the teacher and student. It may represent a period or style of piece not already included in the examination program, but which holds special interest for the candidate. The choice must be within the following guidelines:

1) The equivalent level of difficulty of the piece may be at a higher grade level, providing it is within the technical and musical grasp of the candidate.

2) Pieces below the equivalent of Grade 9 level of difficulty are not acceptable.

3) The piece must be for solo guitar. Duets and trios are not acceptable.

4) Candidates with exceptional talent for improvisation may wish to improvise upon a theme of their choice. In this case, items 1 and 2 (above) will apply. Marks will be given for originality, musical inventiveness, and structural unity.

5) Candidates may choose to play a piece of music from standard real book form chosen either from any "Fake" Book or from *40 Compositions in Standard Real Form*. In this case, items 1 and 2 (above) will apply. Candidates must play both the melody and a suitable accompaniment. Marks will be given for a stylistic performance.

Special approval is not required for the Supplementary Piece. However, poor suitability of the choice may be reflected in the mark. Memorization is encouraged, though NOT required.

Technical Tests

Conservatory Canada's booklet *Guitar Technique Book* (1999) contains notational examples for all technical requirements.

All technical tests must be played from memory, evenly, with good tone, logical fingering. Metronome markings should be regarded as *minimum* speeds. The number of octaves are as given in *Guitar Technique Book* (1999).

KEYS REQUIRED IN GRADE TEN

	Keys
Major	ALL Keys
Minor	ALL Keys

SCALES

To be played from memory, ascending AND descending, in the keys stated.

Scale fingerings: Right hand, fingered i-m, m-a, and i-a (to be specified by the examiner), using rest and free stroke. Use only movable, closed string left-hand fingering (except open 6th string).

	Keys	*M.M.* $\bullet$ =	*Articulation*
Major	All keys	112 112	in sixteenth notes AND in triplet eighth notes
Minor (Harmonic AND Melodic)	All keys	112 112	in sixteenth notes AND in triplet eighth notes
Repeated	All keys	84	in quintuplet sixteenth notes AND in sextuplet sixteenth notes
Slur	G, A	144	in compound triplet eighth notes
3rd & 6th	A	104	solid in eighth notes AND broken in sixteenth notes
Chromatic	beginning on E	112 112	in sixteenth notes AND in triplet eighth notes

Note: Do NOT repeat the upper tonic note.
Do NOT play either the tonic chord or a cadence at the end of the scale.

ARPEGGIOS

To be played ascending AND descending in the keys stated.

	Keys	*Position*	*M.M.* $\bullet$ =	*Note Values*
Major	All keys		104	in eighth notes
Minor	All keys		104	in eighth notes
Dominant 7th	All keys (Major and Minor)		104	in eighth notes
Diminished 7th	All Minor keys		104	in eighth notes

HARMONIZATION
Candidates are required to harmonize a simple melody at sight. Candidates are expected to play both the melody AND an appropriate accompaniment in at least a two-voice texture. Use of unessential tones in the accompaniment is encouraged but not required. No indication of chord of chord changes will be given.

Keys of   A, E, F Major
              f#,d, Minor
Chords   I, i, IV, iv, V or V^7 (root and first inversion)
              ii and vi chords may be used but are not required.

Example

Sight Reading

Candidates are required to perform at sight a) a rhythmic exercise and b) a passage of guitar score as described below. The candidate will be given a brief period to scan the score, but not to "practise silently" before beginning to play. Candidates must perform each section without counting aloud. It is recommended that candidates maintain a steady beat, and avoid the unnecessary repetition caused by attempting to correct errors during the performance.

Rhythm	*Guitar Passage*
To tap, clap or play on one note (at the candidate's choice) a rhythm in simple or compound time. May include syncopated rhythms, changing-meters, irregular meters, and complex patterns.	To play at sight a short guitar piece equal in difficulty to pieces of Grade 6-7 level, in any style or period. May include modulations, changing meters and irregular meters
Length 4-8 bars	Keys Major & Minor ALL keys
Time signature any simple or compound time	Length 16-32 bars
Note values variety of values including ties	
Rest values variety of values	

Example: a) Rhythm

Aural Tests

The candidate will be required:

i)   at the candidate's choice, to play back OR sing back to any vowel, the **lower** part of a two-part phrase in a major key, after the Examiner has:
         ✓named the key [up to and including three sharps or flats]
         ✓played the 4-note chord on the tonic in solid form
         ✓played the passage twice.

The parts may begin on ANY note of the tonic chord. Following is the approximate level of difficulty:

ii) to identify any of the following intervals after the Examiner has played each one once. Intervals may be played in melodic (broken) form OR harmonic (solid) form.

ABOVE a note
major and minor 2nd
major and minor 3rd
perfect 4th
augmented 4th (diminished 5th)
perfect 5th
major and minor 6th
major and minor 7th
perfect octave

BELOW a note
major and minor 2nd
major and minor 3rd
perfect 4th
augmented 4th (diminished 5th)
perfect 5th
major and minor 6th
major and minor 7th
perfect octave

iii) to identify any of the following 4-note chords after each has been played once by the Examiner.

major and *minor* chords: root position and first or second inversion [to be played in solid form, close position]

dominant 7th chords: root position or any inversion [to be played in solid form, close position]

diminished 7th chords: root position only [to be played in solid form, open (SATB) position]

iv) to state whether a short piece in *chorale* style is in a *major* or a *minor* key, and whether the final cadence and all internal cadences are *Perfect* (V-I), *Imperfect* (I-V, II-V, IV-V), *Plagal* (IV-I), or *Interrupted/Deceptive* (V-VI). The Examiner will play the passage TWICE; the first time straight through without interruption, the second time stopping at cadence points for the candidate to identify them.

RECITAL ASSESSMENT

Recital Assessments are NOT FOR GRADED CREDIT.

The Recital Assessment is offered in most Practical disciplines, at the follow levels:

I. JUNIOR (Grades 1 to 4)

Duration of the recital:	20 minutes (maximum) of music
Registration Fee:	Please consult the current examination application form for the schedule of fees.
Prerequisites:	None

II. INTERMEDIATE (Grades 5 to 8)

Duration of the recital:	30 minutes (maximum) of music
Registration Fee:	Please consult the current examination application form for the schedule of fees.
Prerequisites:	None

III. SENIOR (Grades 9-10)

Duration of the recital:	40 minutes (maximum) of music
Registration Fee:	Please consult the current examination application form for the schedule of fees.
Prerequisites:	None

Each level may be taken as many times as desired.

The Recital Assessment takes the form of a short recital that is open to the public, free of charge. It is intended to offer students an alternative to regular graded examinations, and to encourage development of performance skills, including program selection and stage deportment. Its significant benefits include a defined, but flexible goal, and the critique of the Examiner, an experienced professional musician.

The Recital Assessment does not replace regular graded examinations, but can be a valuable supplement and stimulus to musical studies and repertoire development. The assessment focuses entirely on performance; no testing of technical or aural skills is required.

Repertoire should be chosen from the List Pieces and/or Study Lists in the Conservatory Syllabus, at or around the candidate's grade level. The program may include a maximum of TWO pieces not on the Syllabus Lists. You may include a maximum of ONE piece using an instrumental obbligato. Irregular list approval is not required for any of your pieces.

The program should be chosen with due regard for artistic and technical style, variety and balance. It is not essential that the recital program include works from every musical period or syllabus list category. Verbal introduction of some or all pieces (though not required), will serve both to demonstrate the candidate's background knowledge and to develop rapport with the audience.

The Examiner will give a written assessment of the performance along with a classification of the standard (i.e., distinction, honours, pass, etc.). However, no mark will be given. A Certificate of Participation will be awarded to candidates who achieve the minimum standard of "Pass" or above. The Examiner will base the assessment as follows:

Choice of program	10%
Stage deportment	10%
Musical performance	80%